CANCER - A MAGICAL QUEST

Patricia Walsh

First published and distributed from the UK in 2020
by Patricia Walsh, self-publishing author

© Patricia Walsh 2020

The moral right of the author has been asserted

All rights reserved. This book may not be reproduced in whole or in part without written permission from the author, except by a reviewer who may quote brief passages in a review. Nor may any part or whole of this book be reproduced, stored in a retrieval system, or transmitted, or otherwise be copied for public or private use, in any form or by any means, electronic, mechanical, photocopying, recording or other, without the written permission from the publisher. Nor may it be otherwise circulated in any form of binding or cover other than that in which it is published and without a similar condition being posed on the subsequent purchaser.

The information given in this book should not be treated as a substitute for professional medical advice, always consult a medical practitioner or specialist. Any use of the information contained in this book is at the reader's discretion and risk. The author cannot be held responsible for any loss, claim or damage arising out of the use, or misuse, of the suggestions made, the failure to take medical advice or for any material on third party websites.

In 2014 Patricia was diagnosed with cancer and for personal reasons she chose not to undergo conventional therapy. Her search to find another possibility led her to the path of Traditional Chinese Medicine (TCM). Having found a skilled practitioner, the journey to recovery began. Deep in meditation, while receiving acupuncture, a door to the infinite was about to open. In order to access the door it meant going first to the heart to find once again a place of trust and love. At the doorway, the conditioned self and ego must be left behind. On the other side of the door lay the world of stillness - darkness – the void - the very core of one's being. In this place, all fears are released, including that of death. Here one finds the self, with endless possibilities - the universe within and a sense of returning home.

About the Author

Patricia Walsh is an intuitive counsellor, currently working for a London rape crisis centre. She has over 10 years' experience working in refuges, outreach work and as an independent domestic violence advisor. Her initial interest in healing took her into the careers of nursing and occupational therapy. Realising that the role of mind in recovery from disease was paramount she then went on to explore the world of psychology, hypnotherapy, and counselling. It was her close encounter with death in 2014 that resulted in a totally different perception and meaning to life, inspiring her to write her autobiography *Cancer – A Magical Quest*. During this time of immense personal growth, she experienced the transformative power of Qigong - an ancient Chinese form of movement, breathing exercises and meditation which was to provide her with the ultimate healing of mind, body and spirit. Her training as a Reiki Practitioner had already introduced her to the importance of energy work in healing and in 2019 she graduated as a teacher from the London College of Elemental Chi Kung (Qigong).

Along with individual counselling, Patricia is also a lead group facilitator running regular self-help groups in Surrey. Using a programme that she devised herself, entitled *The Way of the Goddess*, she invites female survivors of childhood trauma, to challenge their earlier conditioned beliefs and bring about changes in their lives. Motivated by the results of inner child therapy, she is currently working on a new technique of storytelling as an effective and safe method of communication for the clients to express their trauma.

Patricia can be contacted on: thewayofthegoddess1@gmail.com

About the cover

I am so grateful to Mario Duguay for granting me permission to use his beautiful artwork for my book cover. I have owned a set of his cards for more than twenty years and they were particularly pertinent when I was recovering from ill health. Picking a card each day to start my day, uplifted my spirit and I cannot think of a more perfect way to illustrate my quest. I have chosen two from his oracle cards *Messages of Light* because each comes with a message particularly relevant to my quest.

The front cover is named The Path of Light - Life places the perfect people and situations on my path to help me advance on my journey of inner growth. In spite of all obstacles, I have the courage, I become aware of my life's experiences and I study them wisely in order to improve myself. I choose to grow in faith and am confident that, at the end of my road, I will join the Light.

The back cover is named A Door to the Infinite - Inside me is a door to the Infinite. I take the time to go to my heart centre and link up with Heaven. In this serene place, I am eternal and indestructible. Through this inner journey, I am able to see beyond life's challenges and reach the higher levels of my existence. My inner light is my greatest strength and my greatest wealth.

Dedication

I dedicate this book to Christopher, without whom, I would not be alive. Thank you for teaching me how to 'listen', in my quest to heal my mind, body and spirit and above all for taking me on such an exquisitely beautiful journey into Light.

Christopher can be contacted on:
https://www.christopherswoodward.com

In gratitude for my dear friend Agnieszka who has supported me on every step of the journey. My book would not have reached completion without you.

I would like to thank the following:
Sally - my friend, and reiki practitioner, who first showed me how to interpret reiki energy into light and visuals. Jeremy - my Qigong practitioner for a wonderful healing session including a singing bowl and a purring cat. Thalbert - Director & Principal Tutor at CECK , along with his two assistants Susan & Carol for teaching me the essence of Qigong. All the staff at Breast Cancer Haven - particularly Sonia, Edem, Denise and Gosia.

I would like to express my deep appreciation for my two sons, for their love and support. My brother and sisters who assisted me when I most needed it. Annette, for your wonderful friendship - you never forgot a single birthday of mine in more than 40 years and completely understood why I could not take a conventional therapy route. Rosemary - the best travel companion you could find and the only person I know who would accompany me on a trek with a donkey into unknown territory without GPS. Brenda - who first took me into the world of philosophy and a new way of thinking. Etty and Martin for their editing and formatting skills.

For all the amazing clients, with whom I have had the good fortune to meet on their paths to recovery. Your courage and resilience has inspired me throughout my work. You have all taught me so much and in turn your teachings have been passed on to other survivors and we live in hope that eventually the tide will turn and one day, women will no longer need to live in fear.

For my beautiful dog Iona, who showed me what love and loyalty really means. You will remain in my heart forever.

Finally, I would like to acknowledge my abusers who without their abject cruelty and darkness, I may never have reached my full potential and experienced such perfect light.

Contents

About the Author i

About the cover iii

Dedication iv

Contents vii

Introduction 1

Chapter 1 – Early Childhood Experiences 4

Chapter 2 – The Tibetan Monks 20

Chapter 3 – Into the Outside World 31

Chapter 4 – Growth of a Tumour 46

Chapter 5 – Diagnosis 63

Chapter 6 – On the Road to Recovery 73

Chapter 7 – The Importance of Diet and Exercise 83

Chapter 8 – The Haven 91

Chapter 9 – The Fire Element and The Burrotrek 100

Chapter 10 – White Light, the Cosmos and Infinity 108

Chapter 11 – The Primordial Child 115

Chapter 12 – Detachment 123

Chapter 13 – Initiation: Entering into Light 137

Chapter 14 – The Halls of Illusion 145

Chapter 15 – Completion 155

Introduction

'Cancer - A Magical Quest' may seem a strange title for a book, particularly when the word 'cancer' normally strikes an uncontrollable fear and dread into the hearts of most people. When it came to my own diagnosis, I was no exception, particularly as it had claimed the female lives of my mother's entire family and was now working its way through the next generation. My cousin had died of ovarian cancer in her fifties. One of my sisters had been diagnosed with breast cancer two years prior to my diagnosis in May 2014. I had watched my mother when I was 16 years old doing battle with the debilitating effects of surgery and radiotherapy and it was for this very reason that when my turn came, I turned my back and walked away from conventional medicine because it terrified me. When overwhelming things occur in my life, I have never thought of them as a 'coincidence'. I have learnt over the years that when certain forces are at work it is for a reason which generally initiates changes that are necessary and that I am very reluctant to make.

At first, I had called my book 'A Cancer Journey' but in the end it became a quest to find not only an answer to my cancer diagnosis but also its root cause. If I were not to use conventional therapy it would require many changes and dedication to this mission. It began slowly with diet, lifestyle, sleep, avoidance of stress, intuition but perhaps the most significant one of all was what I can only call divine intervention, which presented itself in many different ways. It began in the form of a beautiful sentient being, a Red Setter who we called Iona. We found each other at a time when I needed a good companion to see me through the most difficult period of my life while I was raising my family. She was stunning to look at, funny, mischievous, vivacious, and her joy for living radiated from her lovely big, brown, glowing eyes. Everyone who met her remarked "What a lovely dog!" and she knew on her walks who needed special affection if they were having a down day. When she was not running the fields with joyous abandonment, free from all the restrictions of her lead, she spent her walks looking for old beer cans and plastic bottles and would fastidiously bring them home for recycling as if she knew instinctively what was happening to our beautiful planet. She was my best friend and we loved each other deeply and unconditionally. She looked after me when I was unwell and, just after completing my book, I had to release her soul, freeing her forever from the diseases she had taken on board from those living closely with her. Such was her love for the entire family.

The next intervention that took place on this journey was when I contacted a past acquaintance of mine, Sally, who was trained in reiki. She listened without judgement to my wish to manage my cancer without conventional therapy. It was to be the training ground for a therapist and client to learn to 'communicate' in a completely different way. As she delivered reiki, I learnt to receive in colours, meditation and messages what my body required at that time, even down to the food I needed to eat to help restore its balance. It was the ideal precursor for what was to happen next.

The third and most unexpected meeting was with an extraordinarily gifted acupuncturist, Christopher, at Breast Cancer Haven in London. He is a truly remarkable human being. He understood completely my ability to go into deep meditation and touch higher realms while receiving acupuncture. As he encouraged my life force to return, it would eventually enable me to release my crushed spirit. With a free spirit I could travel through light, the cosmos and infinity discovering a new understanding of consciousness and ultimately a new understanding of myself. It was only then that I realised that the real purpose of this quest was not in finding the 'cure' for my cancer but to find the purpose of my life. As acupuncture and meditation combined, Qigong emerged – an ancient Chinese practice over 5,000 years old. I had an overpowering desire to learn this discipline as I knew it would unlock something beyond my present comprehension. The quest had only just begun. Through this ancient wisdom, I trained first in the basic exercises of elemental Qigong and then discovered by the study of alchemical Qigong that I wasn't just a physical body, but energy in different forms which I was in charge of. It revealed to me that the purpose of my soul was to unite with spirit and to return to the source, having first lit the flame, shared it with others and assisted in the evolution of consciousness, before its final journey back home.

Introduction

This book, therefore, is NOT about 'curing' cancer. We are bombarded by rogue cells being made all day, every day. If the body is not properly maintained or our environment deteriorates around us, either physically, emotionally or both, it is only a matter of time before it may eventually succumb to this disease. More important than the 'cure' is the question that needs to be asked when someone has a cancer diagnosis:

'Do You Want to Live?'

This may sound an odd question to ask when someone is facing the possibility of death, but it is a very important one. If the answer is 'yes', then it is about putting 'intention' into the changes that are needed for a full and vital life. This is different from finding a 'cure' or 'healing'. It is about what I call 'finding what makes your heart sing'. Everyone has to ultimately find their own way of dealing with ill health and the path may require much weeding, replanting and patience. No matter which path you choose, it is not an easy one. Regaining a healthy body, mind and spirit takes time. There are moments when I still find it hard to comprehend why I should be the one who was chosen out of all the millions of people who have cancer to be lined up for such an amazingly beautiful experience but that is exactly what it has been. It was almost as if my ill health was predestined in order to bring these remarkable teachers into my life and where the things of importance that I have studied and learnt throughout this and other lifetimes have now been pieced together like a magnificent puzzle. Each piece has slotted into place with the utmost and exquisite perfection. It is now time to share this wonderful quest and leave behind a map for others, so that this experience is not lost and archived only in my memory for ever.

With precision timing my next divine intervention entered into my life in the form of my precious friend Agnieszka. She has patiently helped me throughout as I struggled with the concepts I was being shown during my therapy sessions and with loving guidance offered me ways to understand. Finally, she read and edited the first drafts of this book and offered suggestions as to how best I might put into words this truly magical quest.

CHAPTER 1

Early Childhood Experiences

Childhood is such an important part of shaping who we are and that is why I find it remarkable that, out of all our vast store of accumulated memories, surprisingly few seem to remain as important 'significant events'. I was born in England to an Irish Catholic family and my perception of the purpose of each child's existence in that family was to work. As more children were produced, until finally a boy was born, each child in turn became a victim of the facade of playing happy families in a completely dysfunctional home. The role of this male when he was born would not only be to bear the family name but to continue the family business.

My earliest memory goes back to the age of two and a half years old when the first major disruption happened in my life. I awoke early one morning to my father explaining to my two older sisters that something had happened to 'Mammy' and she was in hospital and we would all have to manage for a while. It was to be many years later that one of my sisters found out that 'Mammy' had had a miscarriage and lost a baby boy but my mother remained in denial of this throughout her life. Even years later, when I became a mother myself and I explained to her that a friend from my antenatal group had had a miscarriage, she said that fortunately this had never happened to her. It is not my place to judge her because it is easy to be critical when you are not walking in that person's shoes. The pressure to produce a 'son and heir' in such a family was immense, particularly as her younger sister seemed to have no trouble in producing boys. At the time, producing the 'right' sex child was the woman's responsibility and a result of her supposed good

Chapter 1 - Early Childhood Experiences

biology. However, scientifically, it was known even back then, just as it is known now, that this is not the case.

My mother's denial of the miscarriage was a lesson to me about how deep the process of denial can go in order to cope with emotional trauma. It also helped to explain why she was so resentful of me because by the time she came to having her third child, she was hoping that finally her boy would be born and her body could have a rest from childbearing. She had even chosen a boy's name for me and I was going to be even more special because my due date of birth was 17th March. Patrick would be born on St Patrick's Day. Perfect! Except it wasn't - I became Patricia born just minutes after the 17th March and I was the wrong gender. I was to be constantly reminded of this throughout my young life.

"You should have been a boy, you know."

This was to be my mantra.

After what was probably some days it appeared that 'Mammy' was not going to be back anytime soon and so my sisters were sent to stay with my father's sister. Even though his sister lived in the next village, my mother had barely spoken to her over the years so it said a lot for her generosity to take in two additional children into her large family. I was sent to Edna, my friend Pauline's mother, who had recently been in hospital as she had had polio in the past and had additional ongoing physical problems including scoliosis of the spine and walked with the assistance of a calliper. It later transpired that Edna was the person my mother was visiting when she took a tumble coming down the steps of the hospital when she was seven months pregnant and consequently miscarried. This at least was the story my sister prised out of my father many years later.

I enjoyed staying with Pauline. Edna was sweet and kind and the house seemed pleasant and calm with no shouting. In spite of her physical disability, she never seemed to complain about anything even though it took her much longer to go upstairs or bend down to pick things off the floor. This was the first realisation that I had of a very different way to be in a family. I didn't have to hold my breath tightly in case something was about to happen or begin to tremble in fear as voices were raised loudly in anger. I could laugh spontaneously, and Pauline and I could turn the radio up loud and dance together or run up and down the stairs and make a noise. We would look at books and her mother would smile at us and join in the fun and read to us. Unfortunately, I did not stay there for long because my mother's ill health was now going to last much longer than was originally anticipated. A more long-term solution for our accommodation had to be found. We were placed in a Catholic orphanage in the south of England as my father was a self-employed printer and worked day and night in order to keep the ever-growing family so he did not have time to care for us. When I left Pauline's home, she gave me four of her beautiful ballet figurines to take with me as we both, even at that young age, had a passion for dance.

My father took us for one last visit to see my mother before we left. She was on the first floor in a room of her own where she was 'convalescing' and after a quick cuddle with her and a cake from her tea tray I waved my final goodbye from the garden of the grounds of the small hospital and we caught the train to the orphanage.

I do not remember much about the arrival at the orphanage. All we sisters were put together in a little side dormitory and a new life was to begin. Since I was the youngest, I had an older girl assigned to look after me. She was cuddly and warm and taught me to read and my days were full of fun and enjoyment. I loved playing in a big indoor Wendy house and making cups of tea for the dolls and soft toys with no one to bully me. I will call the girl Bertha as I do not recall her name but in my child's mind that is what I remember she was called. I particularly enjoyed weekends because on Saturdays the wooden floors were polished and we would tie dusters to our shoes with large elastic bands, hold hands and skate up and down to make sure the polish was rubbed into the floor and brought a shine to it. It wasn't long before my yellow duster shoes became transformed into soft pink ballet shoes. I would let go of the hands holding me and set off solo across the big dining hall, twirling and sliding my way up and down the floor. I would emulate famous ballerina pirouettes like Pauline and I used to do when we played together. Inevitably someone would lose their balance and we would finish up falling on top of each other and sit on the floor laughing. Whenever I think of the orphanage it is with happy, joyful memories. I had little to do with my sisters other than sharing the room at night to sleep. I felt loved and above all I began to read more and more. My mind would disappear into the fantasies of beautiful fairy stories and the world of imagination and Bertha was always there to help me struggle through the more difficult words until I had a grasp of them. By the age of three I was reading fluently.

For a young child, time has little significance so it was probably about six months later that my sisters and I were called to the office. I

Chapter 1 - Early Childhood Experiences

remember the large heavy oak door and the vast room with high, white embossed ceilings. This was where my father had taken us on the first day. Bertha got me dressed in a plain blue dress piped with a white broderie anglaise trim. It was my favourite dress and she always plaited my hair. On this day she pinned my plaits up across my head like the pictures I had seen in the *Heidi* books. She told me I was going to meet my mother and father and I was going to go home. I did not at this stage have any memory of my mother and I certainly didn't know where home was since this was now the only home I knew. I felt extremely frightened and asked her questions as she led me by the hand and took me inside. I looked at the two strangers before me sitting on high-backed chairs that looked like thrones. The man was dressed in a brown suit and I gradually recognised his features as that of my father as he had visited us a few times during our stay. The lady seemed a complete stranger. She had on a beautiful navy pinstriped suit, a pretty, lacy, white blouse and a little pill box hat. She looked very smart and she beckoned me to come over and sat me on her lap. I assumed this was my mother and gradually something about her smell must have evoked memories as I sat on her lap and she held me close. After a short conversation, we all got up to leave to catch the train back 'home'.

The train journey was particularly memorable as I wanted to go to the toilet but I was too frightened to cross the carriage divides to get there. In those days, you could see down onto the tracks as the train moved and I was terrified I would fall down onto them as they went whizzing by below me. I must have become more and more fidgety until my sister announced proudly to my mother and most of the carriage that I had wet myself. This was not actually the case but this was to be the start of learning to hold back tears of shame and embarrassment.

Once back 'home', my life was to change forever. It was dysfunctional and violent and I learnt fear, rejection and an ability to remain as quiet as possible in order to try to avoid the continual chastisement from my mother. As a young vulnerable child, like the experiment with Pavlov's dogs, I was an ideal candidate for conditioning. Aristotle's famous quote "Give me a child until he is 7 and I will show you the man" could have been written for me. Long before I was 7, I learnt that I was no good, I was fat, ugly and I would never amount to anything. Consequently, I began to feel uncomfortable in my body and with who I was. I also had a feeling that none of what was going on around me was real, as if there was a giant mirror between me and the world and that I could see everything outside but I was invisible.

The older I got the worse the violence in the home seemed to get. I do not fully recall the event that led up to one of the worst incidents but I do remember my mother pounding up the stairs, separating my sister from me who was, as usual, punching and taunting me. I was dragged rapidly by my long hair down the stairs backwards and I could feel the pain in my spine as I hit each step along the way. After many such similar occasions, I had learnt to mentally count the steps down so that I would know how many were left to go. At the bottom of the stairs was an ugly brown wooden electricity cupboard that, although small and narrow, jutted out from the wall and had sharp corners. I closed my eyes tightly and prayed that my eyes would not strike the edge. My biggest fear was that if I had no eyes, how would I ever read again? Past the electricity cupboard I bounced to the frosted glass front door straight ahead. You could not see out and no one could see in. This was the next danger zone as I visualised what would happen if I went through the glass. My face would be cut to pieces and I might be left looking like a monster. I prayed that this would not happen. My high-speed descent finished with a short journey along the hall and into the lounge. My sister hot footed it down the stairs to join in and I was then kicked like a football around the lounge floor. I covered my head with my arms to avoid the blows to my face and I curled up to avoid the kicks in the stomach but this then left my back, arms and legs painfully exposed.

Suddenly, an extraordinary event took place. The next thing I knew was that I was looking down from the ceiling viewing my body on the floor that was still being kicked but I could feel no pain! I was no longer afraid and a feeling of excitement came over me and my heart was pounding. Then a thought occurred to me: 'Was I dead?' If I wasn't in my body and I couldn't feel anything I must be dead. They had killed me. When I thought about this, I didn't mind at all. A huge sense of relief washed over me, never to have to be hurt or shouted at again. How wonderful that would be. Floating around, up on the ceiling and watching them like an angel seemed a much more beautiful option. I wondered if they opened the window if I might float off out into the air like the butterflies or even higher with the birds, up and beyond into a world of mists. All of a sudden, the shouting became louder and the physical attack became more ferocious.

"Look at her! She won't even cry! The little bitch!" my mother screamed. "Go on cry, cry!"

I wondered how you could cry and produce tears if you were no longer in your body. The assault was getting worse and then suddenly I

Chapter 1 - Early Childhood Experiences

arrived very rapidly back into my body. It was a shock and I became aware of feeling sore and exhausted. Eventually, my mother's rage was spent even though I could not produce tears to please her. I lay for a while crushed and broken on the floor. She then shouted at me to get up off the floor and began talking about what she needed to get done as if nothing untoward had happened. I would have been nearly five years old at this time and these beatings were to be a regular part of my childhood – as were my out-of-body experiences (OBEs).

I always felt much older than my years as though sometimes I knew much more than other people even though I was considered a child and a pretty stupid one at that. These events that happen in childhood are the reason why adults of childhood abuse find it so difficult to report against their perpetrators. They learn to normalise these experiences just as the adult normalises it as if it is part of life to put your child into a life-threatening situation, kick and punch it like a prize boxer and then talk about going to do the shopping! Had I not experienced these events first hand, I do not think that I would have had the understanding that I have today when the clients I work with express their views about feeling confused as to why they allowed such things to happen to them.

Eventually, I would have OBEs spontaneously. Sometimes while travelling on a train. I would suddenly find myself doing some remote viewing of the entire carriage as we travelled. I found it fascinating that I could see everyone sitting in their seats. Having overcome my fear of falling down onto the tracks I would pretend to my mother that I was visiting the toilet to check if what I had seen from above was really true ... and it was. The people were exactly as I had seen them while remote viewing. I had learnt by now to keep the joy of what I was experiencing to myself as the repercussions would have been huge.

Although for the most part my childhood was like a heavy November day, occasionally a timid sun would shine through which fortunately had a lasting effect on me as I grew up and later would become instrumental in my recovery from ill health. After we left the orphanage, we went on a holiday to Ireland to 'visit the relatives'. I did not see very much of my mother during this holiday and I was looked after by her step-mother, Norah. My mother had no love for Norah as her own mother had died when she was only 12 and she and her sister had been sent to boarding school in Leeds. My mother always felt that they were rejected so her father could have time with Norah before he decided to re-marry. Noni, as she was affectionately known, was always a busy lady looking after the large farm. She never seemed to dress in anything else but her working clothes and an apron over the top, except of course for Sunday Mass. She had a homely smell of soda bread, cows and warm farm kitchens. Soon we developed a special bond. She cared for her animals with a passion, particularly the many dogs that were kept on the farm. Once the farm hands were all fed, she would take out all the dog bowls and fill them with exactly the same meals that the farm hands had had. Generally, they had boiled bacon or lamb, cabbage, potatoes and gravy. She would then call them into the kitchen and made sure they all ate their own dinners and one didn't get more than another. Gradually she gave me the task of calling them all in and I delighted in watching these wonderful creatures wag their tails and rush into the kitchen. They were so full of fun and energy and even the 'auld ones' were bounding with vigour. Having finished their dinners, they would gather round Noni and out they would come with their big licky pink tongues and shower her hands in kisses of thanks and affection. I was smitten with them. In hindsight it is interesting to note that dogs didn't seem to go to vets in those days unless they were severely injured. They ate fresh food and roamed freely around the land. Their 'walk' was to run through the fields with the farmer and I doubt they were ever vaccinated. I am sure there were some who were neglected by their owners particularly in Southern Ireland, which is not known for its pet welfare. However, when treated well with fresh food, open space, and a lack of medical intervention, it probably meant that their lives were a lot healthier than today with the use of processed foods, vaccinations and antibiotics. They certainly didn't seem to have the incidents of malignant tumours at a young age that we are seeing nowadays.

As the holiday came to the halfway point, there were a few more memorable days that still stay with me. I was sitting outside the front porch of Noni's house with the warm sunshine all around me. I had some knitting needles and a ball of red wool and two stitches that were going nowhere. My mother had set me up with about ten originally and then went off walking in the fields. I wanted to learn to knit more than anything because I had seen the beautiful Fair Isle waistcoats she had made for my father and bright yellow matinee coats that she knitted for other people's babies. It fascinated me how such beautiful colours and designs could come from two needles and balls of wool. Noni came out to see what I was doing and she laughed when she saw my two stitches and my sad face as the stitches just disappeared every time I twisted the wool through them. She stood behind me and holding my hands firmly in hers she showed me exactly what I needed to do with my hands and

Chapter 1 - Early Childhood Experiences

the yarn. In a short time, she had taught me and I even figured out what to do on my own when a stitch dropped down. I loved this craft and before long I was knitting my own sweaters and eventually went on as an adult to knit Fair Isle and Shetland designs. I also learnt spinning, natural dying and weaving.

This holiday, away from home, was wonderful but my sister always seemed to find a way to spoil things for me, such as finding my mother's bright red lipstick and trying it on and then accidentally getting it on my mother's best white blouse. It always became my fault no matter what. I could have been in Timbuktu at the time but the blame would still be apportioned to me. It was interesting to study in later life the different coping mechanisms that children adopt when they are brought up in abusive homes including colluding with the perpetrator in order to win favours and keep themselves safe. They collaborate with the adult rather like many people collaborated with the enemy when their countries were invaded during the Second World War. As a child, you do not know any differently and the priority is to save your own skin.

During that holiday, we also visited my father's home and stayed on the farm there. Grandma would feed the chickens and let me help her and she would put saucers of fresh cow's milk down for two amazing looking cats. They were white with red eyes and a pink hue to their ears. I was somewhat in awe of them at first as I thought they were magical creatures and must have come from another planet. I adored this world of beautiful animals, and the great big horse that ploughed the field, and the smell of their bodies was like no scent I had ever smelt before. This gift of the ability to smell nature is still with me now. I can smell when my dog gets ill even before she manifests an illness. Before I left, my grandmother gave me a pull-along dog that had come from America. He was made of wood and clicked as you led him around. He had a bell around his neck and soft felt ears and his name was Butch, which was written on the collar around his neck. I still have him to this day. He became the best friend I ever had as a child and I cuddled him so much his ears fell off!

At the end of the holiday, we went to visit a seaside resort called Ballybunion and this was the first time I had ever seen the sea. I remember feeling so excited even though it was a cold day. Irish mothers had a very strange ritual in those days. The girl children had to have their hair specially washed and put into ringlets and dressed in their best clothes for a grand day out! If you were lucky you got to take your shoes and socks off and walk barefoot on the sand. The boys, however, wore shorts and open-toed sandals and could roll in the sand and paddle in the sea as much as they liked. Sandwiches fit to feed an army were packed up and my grandfather was looking forward to his feast of winkles bought on the sea front and handed to him in a small paper bag. He had a pin in his coat lapel especially for the job in hand and I remember him putting one of these revolting, salty, blubbery things in my mouth, having carefully picked it out of its shell with the pin. It tasted of salt, sand and grit and the texture was disgusting and it was so difficult to swallow it down so as not to offend him or make me feel I had wasted one of his precious tasty morsels. It was another example of learning to please others because you were expected to. On that same day, as I looked out over the horizon into the vast expanse of ocean, I could see tiny little silver, sparkly corkscrews dancing off the sea. Soon I was aware of them all around me as they sparkled, danced and collided with each other. They were in the sea, on the sand, in the air, absolutely everywhere. I became so excited jumping up and down and pointing at them. I tried to catch them but I couldn't because they couldn't be held. I didn't know what they were so I didn't have a name for them. I pointed them out to my mother, who clearly couldn't see them and when I told her they were silver zizzy things she decided that they were splashes from the waves. I knew this was not the case and I felt disappointed that no one else could see them or could tell me what they were. In my mind I called them zizzy things and later, when I came home, I could see them in the water when the bath was running. There seemed to be more of them on a sunny day and they would fill the whole bathroom. My mother decided they were just dust particles in the air but I knew what dust particles looked like. Very soon I learnt that these could not be talked about as it made my mother very angry, probably because I became very animated and emptied half the bath water onto the floor, and for her it was yet another one of my fantastic illusions. It was to be more than fifty years later before my zizzy things were given the name of 'chi' in such a matter of fact way that there appeared to be nothing out of this world about it. I was reassured that it was quite normal to see it at the sea and in fast running water.

All too soon, the holiday came to an end and we returned to England. My eldest sister was periodically included in the assaults from time to time but she was always incredibly smart and by the time she reached the age of about twelve she had learnt how to deal with it. She lay on the floor one day and feigned an epileptic fit and my mother was so worried an ambulance might have to be called that, from that day on,

Chapter 1 - Early Childhood Experiences

my sister was mostly no longer part of the physical violence, although she did have to listen to the noise while she was trying to study. My other sister did not totally escape either and when my mother chose to, labelled her as a trouble maker and left my father to deal with her. I was rarely hit by my father because I was his little 'male' helper around the house for the DIY, but my sister had her fair amount of thrashings from him. One night in her late teens when she had stayed out at an all-night party, she came home and locked herself in the bedroom we both shared. He rushed up the stairs and literally broke the handle, lock and all from the door, arrived like a bull through it and launched his punches on her. Since I shared a double bed with her at that time, I received almost as many blows as she did. One of the things that gave me strength was a small picture postcard of a cartoon bloodhound that, on one of my mother's kinder days, she had allowed me to stick on the bedroom wall. I used to go to bed cuddling myself and imagining what it would be like to cuddle up to one of Noni's dogs or that my postcard had come to life and I could bury my head into its fur and cry all the tears I had into his warm body. After a while this did not escape ridicule and there was a threat by my sister to remove it, particularly as it was in the way of something far more important in life, namely a Mick Jagger poster. It was declared that all girls fancied him and if you didn't there was something wrong with you. Clearly, there was something very wrong with me as my dog was infinitely more appealing than Mick Jagger. I eventually removed him from the wall before someone else did. Every birthday and Christmas, I was asked what I wanted and I always replied:
"A dog."

Consequently, there were a few cuddly dogs at the bottom of my bed and I could at least imagine what the real version might feel like. My favourite was big and brown and was a nightdress case but one night I vomited all over it and when I asked where he was, I was told it was in the bin because I had been sick all over it. I was heartbroken that my favourite dog had gone to the dump and I felt shame and guilt that I had allowed this to happen to him. For me he was real in this awful world of abuse. This too was a useful lesson for the future as I learnt that it is not unusual for female adult survivors of domestic abuse to have a very close bond with animals since the 'love' they receive from an abusive adult is extremely flawed and not to be trusted. It is a way of receiving the unconditional love that they are looking for and it is reciprocal. How cruel our present system is to expect women to move to a refuge with their children, giving up their home and above all their pets because it is so difficult to get adequate pet fostering for an indefinite amount of time. It seems to be that women must always bear ongoing trauma for other people's violent behaviour.

Eventually it was time to go to school. I attended the local Catholic school and there I found it very difficult to make friends. On the first day, I ran away and climbed one of the trees in the large grounds and came down when I saw everyone go back home. Unfortunately, when I arrived home my dress was covered in green stains and I had also dared to remove the ridiculous bows attached to each side of my head which looked like giant butterflies. Each morning the hair ritual happened and at night my hair was twirled around rags to create ringlets which appeared to be mainly a fashion with my mother and no one else. No matter how she tried to curl it, it simply didn't stay for long even when she doused it in hair spray which came at you with such a speed and volume out of the can that you felt like you were being gassed! I begged to have my hair in plaits like all the other girls but was told this was low and common.

On the rare occasion I went to people's homes for parties I felt strange and out of place. I 'knew' my home was very different from others and we were never able to offer an invite back so eventually I became isolated and was rarely given an invitation. Whenever I did go to a party I inevitably came back and vomited and was chastised by my mother for eating potted fish paste sandwiches. I think I vomited out of sheer tension as I could feel my stomach getting tighter; later on in life, I learnt to store most of my stress in the abdominal area. The same is true of many women in domestic abuse situations who are told they are suffering from irritable bowel syndrome. Consequently, the parties usually resulted in the sheets being stripped off the bed in the middle of the night and put to soak, my face and body being roughly cleaned with a face flannel and I was left to shiver naked on the landing while some clean pyjamas were found for me. This was only after the bed was made up first so that I was punished for what I had done. I later mentally made a vow that if ever I had children and they were sick, I would never treat them in such a cruel way. When I did become a mother, I always wrapped my children in warm towels and kissed them and reassured them that the sickness would pass and that it was part of life. However, I forgot to give myself the same reassurance.

Apart from feeling lonely at junior school, it passed fairly uneventfully except for moments of ridicule with certain teachers. One was Miss Fitzmorris, a middle-aged woman dressed in a scratchy wool

Chapter 1 - Early Childhood Experiences

tweed suite and brown brogues. She taught English and her job was to ensure everyone could spell. By this time, I was called 'Cinderella' at home and my job was to clean dishes and help cut vegetables when I returned home from school. Since I was not a boy and I was never going to amount to anything there seemed little point in spending too much time with school and I might as well be 'useful'. Consequently, learning spellings rarely happened and I used to try to cram them into my head while doing the dishes or on the way to school in the morning before the lesson. As they became more difficult, I didn't have enough time to learn them so inevitably one day I arrived and got 6/10 for the test. This was the lowest score in the class so Miss Fitzmorris took great delight in taking the dunce of the spelling test to be shown up as an example and made me climb up on my desk and stand on it for all to view. Here I stood for the remainder of the class. Next morning, I was designated the corner of the classroom to stand in until a more appropriate dunce took over. I was determined that this type of humiliation would never happen again, so, with what little pocket money I was given for the chores, I bought a torch and batteries. There under the bed clothes at night, I learnt my spellings before falling asleep. Not only that, I read books from school and my happy days of the orphanage came back to life, by escaping more and more into books. I read Hans Christian Andersen over and over again: 'The Little Mermaid', 'The Red Shoes' and then, my all-time favourite, 'The Emperor's New Clothes'. I marvelled at the child who had the courage to get up and say what no one dared to say: that the Emperor had nothing on at all! Nowadays not many children have heard this story and I use it in my motivational work with women to illustrate the difficulties of a child trying to express themselves in a world of adult deceit. In the 'real' world, there was one book that took precedence over all others in the Catholic school. This was the Catechism. Like Chairman Mao's *Little Red Book*, we recited it daily. Such questions were posed to you as:

"What is God?"
Answer: *"God is a Supreme Spirit."*
Question: *"Why did God make you?"*
Answer: *"God made me to know him, love him and be happy with him forever in the next."*

Because this was chanted, the words sometimes ran in to each other and 'foreverinthenext' became a word of great intrigue. I wondered what this word meant and most of all what a Supreme Spirit meant. The one that was most scary was the three aspects of God - God the Father, God the Son and God the Holy Ghost. The Holy Ghost was depicted as a large bird glowing and coming out of the sky. I hoped and prayed I never saw it! The Catechism was followed up by weekly Sunday visits to Mass where I would sit and pass the time by mentally swapping which ladies' hats would go best with someone else's coat.

One day on the way back from Mass, we passed the Clarks shoe shop and there in the window were the most beautiful red shoes I had ever seen. I pointed them out to 'Mammy' and she agreed they were lovely and we would have to see what Father Christmas might bring. Although my mother was violent there were beautiful aspects to her. She was extremely generous and if she could make people happy by buying things for them, then that was no doubt her way of expressing love. She would say that she never had two pennies to rub together but she did her utmost to clothe and feed us to the best of her ability. She rarely spent anything on herself and always lived with the fear that if she was ever run over, people would think badly of her that her knickers were held together at the waist by a safety pin. I always found this rather funny as to why you would care about what your knickers looked like if you had been run over! The red shoes came my way for Christmas and I spent the entire walk to the church on Christmas morning re-enacting the story of the 'Red Shoes'. I don't think I have ever enjoyed a trip to the church so much, dancing and skipping my way imagining that the shoes had spells on them and they would never stop dancing, taking me over the hills and far away. Maybe some wild geese might come along and transport me high over the trees into a faraway land. My fantasy world knew no boundaries.

On the subject of dance, shortly after the red shoes, into my life came my father's sister from America - Aunt Josie. She was like a breath of fresh air although my mother didn't seem to think so. She seemed to have an avid dislike and jealousy of all the females in my father's family. Aunt Josie arrived in our house like Father Christmas, bearing a bag of gifts for all of us. To my delight, she brought me what was known as 'a twist dress'. It was named after the dance and the design was straight down and made up of large pink and white stripes and tassels around the bottom. I was also given a beautiful soft girly pink matching cardigan. It was the first time I was not dressed like my sisters. We usually looked like ever taller clones of one another. We were all dressed just the same and since I was being given the hand-me-downs that two people had worn already, by the time they reached me they were shabby and worn. It was so beautiful that I even wanted to wear it in bed. Auntie Josie

Chapter 1 - Early Childhood Experiences

asked me what else I would most like if I could make a wish and I said that I wanted to learn to dance like a ballerina. She gave strict instructions to my mother when she left and gave her money to buy me ballet shoes, a leotard and dance lessons. I was so excited when I started my first term and learnt the five positions of ballet and to do pliés at the barre. I still remember the chords of beautiful classical music that the pianist played as we began our exercises. I was transported to another world and the chains that held my spirit were broken. I felt the dance not only in my feet but in my entire body especially when we did freestyle dance at the end of the lesson where we would pretend we were a tree being blown around in the wind or a river flowing down a mountainside. Occasionally, I noticed that some of the girls were looking at me and when I looked at myself in the mirror, I could see the assorted hues of yellow and purple on my back where my bruises were going through their various stages of repair. I chose not to let it affect me. When one girl plucked up the courage to ask, I proudly announced, "I fell off my bike". It made me feel very clever that I had thought of a solution and they must have thought that I was rich if I owned a bike. I neither owned a bike nor a decent uniform but that no longer mattered to me. I could DANCE! However, it wasn't long before that came to an end. It was coming up to half-term and I was called to the Reverend Mother's office and was told I was to do no more dance classes until the school had spoken with my mother. This they dutifully did and I never attended another class again. My mother had been informed that it did not matter who was supplying the money. Dance was an extra-curricular activity and was classified as a luxury and since she was only paying half a crown towards the school fees, the remainder of the money for the ballet classes would go towards my school fees for that term. Now there was nothing more to look forward to.

As the dark physical world closed around me, my higher self was clearly watching on with its master plan. Around the age of seven I began to see 'people' at the bottom of my bed and I would chat to them. Many psychiatrists refer to these as 'imaginary friends', probably caused by severe psychological trauma, but I do not consider this to be the case. Once there was a young girl, a little bit older than me, called Linda. She was dressed in modern-day clothes but there were others who would come too. There was a lady in a long brown dress and a white elasticated cap like those worn by a scullery maid. She looked like the pictures in books describing the time of Florence Nightingale. In view of my abilities later to be able to see into other dimensions, I think I was being comforted from the spirit world. One night my mother overheard me talking aloud when I should have been asleep. She burst through the door, rained down several blows on my body in the bed and told me I was a nutcase. She announced that she would be looking for a psychiatrist if I did not stop and then she would be rid of me as I would be locked up in a psychiatric hospital. I had made the mistake of telling her that I was not talking to myself as she had implied but was talking to the people at the bottom of my bed. I became very worried about this psychiatric hospital and the people in them. It sounded a very big and scary word and might be a place where I would disappear forever since you were locked in and you might never be found again. So I learnt to shut these people out and gradually they no longer appeared. At around this same period in my life, my younger sister was born and so for a while my mother was taken up with the new arrival. She did not seem to have the same disappointment regarding her even though yet another girl was born. My mother kept saying how frail she was and it was a miracle she was born at all as she was lying across her rather than head down. If it wasn't for the intervention of Dr Watt, our GP, and Mother Mary, neither my mother nor the baby would be alive. Shortly after the birth she was all dressed up one day in a black suit and smart hat and she said she was going off to the church to be 'churched'. I remember asking her what this meant and she replied that when you had a baby you had to go and be cleansed because you had brought a baby into the world with original sin. I wanted to know what this original sin was and if everyone was born with it and how they would cleanse her. I was told that babies were born from an unclean act and this would be dealt with by holy water. I imagined her best suit being spoilt by having to have a bath in the water or maybe she went to a big bath tub at the church. This was the kind of religious indoctrination that was given to women, not only about their sexuality but also about giving birth and why Jesus could be nothing other than a virgin birth.

As my sister grew older, I was left to my own devices and my mother enhanced my isolation by telling me that now I was the middle one, I was too young for the older children and too old for the younger one. During the summer months, my job was to tend the vegetables in the garden and pick the many blackcurrants which were at the top of the garden. The best ones grew under the shade of an apple tree. I enjoyed the smell of them although they were very bitter and it was an opportunity to talk to the birds and practise my ballet steps, which I had never forgotten. I would also sing having learnt the words to the pop songs that my mother listened to on the radio. My mother indulged herself in cleaning the house until it

Chapter 1 - Early Childhood Experiences

was spotless and displaying four daughters each turned out clean and neat. Physically as we opened our front door to the outside world, we were the perfect family. Clean, neat and orderly. Once the doors closed, emotionally it was like a dungeon – cold, dark and foreboding.

By the time I was nine years old, my brother was finally born and my mother was over the moon. I remember my father having lots to drink and he smiled and laughed a lot and my mother also seemed happy. I particularly loved my brother; he seemed special, not just because he was a boy but because my mother gave me the job of looking after him and playing with him. As he got to toddler age, she would send me upstairs at night to comfort him when she was too tired to do this herself. I would lift him out of his cot and sit him on my lap and cuddle him until he fell asleep. He was so beautiful and soft and innocent with his little hands wrapped around mine. I wondered if he knew what world he had arrived into. It was hardly surprising that years later he told me that he thought I was his mother.

There was one last awful incident that was to shape my life. One of my family members was sexually assaulted as a child. The perpetrator was an upright pillar of society and had children at the local convent school, giving him perfect access to young children. It clearly didn't enter my parents' heads to even report it, probably due to shame as it was a 'dirty' thing to have to report. It was 'normalised' like our own abuse and never spoken about again. When I think back on this incident, it makes me realise how many more children have yet to come forward. We are only currently dealing with the tip of the iceberg – all those young children's lives devastated by abuse and the amount of mental illness in the society that GPs and NHS workers are not yet fully making the link with.

Life can be a very strange phenomenon. Throughout its time span there appear to come your way, random episodes of what appear to be pieces of a jigsaw. In these early years, I dealt with abuse on every level, abandonment and rejection of the female, and introduced into a strange religious form of indoctrination. Yet on another level I was being guided into the world of out-of-body experiences, the ability to see into other dimensions of the spirit world, the discovery of the magic of chi, reading, dance and the expression of the soul, coloured yarns and the creation of visual splendour, and the pure unconditional love of animals, especially dogs. As yet there were no clues or pictures as to how to put them all together. One day, many years on from these childhood days, they would all make sense and form an amazing picture, but a masterpiece can take a long time and mine was no exception.

ॐ

CHAPTER 2

The Tibetan Monks

I am not quite sure why my mother was prepared to pay a small sum for me to go to the secondary Catholic school but I am very grateful that she did. It was equivalent to a Grammar school and free entry was only by passing the Eleven Plus exam, which entitled the pupil to a free scholarship to the school. My oldest sister did not pass this exam but my mother was determined to send her to a 'good school'. The nuns at that time would have been happy to take her for free if my mother signed her up to be a novitiate. Since Catholics usually had large families and no money to pay for the school fees, if they hadn't passed the exam this was an ideal way to ensure that they paid back in kind with a steady stream of nuns for the future. Fortunately, my mother declined this as an option as she said she could not decide her daughter's future at such a young age even though in traditional Irish Catholic families it was expected that at least one girl would become a nun and one boy would become a priest.

Like my eldest sister, I failed the entrance exam and the alternative was a secondary modern school where you were given the worst education by the worst teachers and then served your time usually as a hairdresser until 'Mr Right' swept you off your feet. Generally, the trend was to get pregnant first and so if it wasn't Mr Right who had fathered the baby, you were stuck with him anyway except in the case of him running off. For the girl, she was looked upon as a slut and a disgrace unless she could be whisked up the aisle before the bump got too large to disclose under her white virginal dress. I dreaded the idea of going to such a school as I couldn't imagine who would want to marry me anyway. I was repeatedly told I was fat - though looking back on the family photos I can see no evidence of that. My career path had already been planned by my mother. My job was going to be the person who put the sweets into a paper bag after they had been weighed out by someone far more able at Woolworth's sweet counter. I was too 'thick' to even be considered for weighing out the sweets, which was done on scales using round individual metal weights. So it came as a great surprise when I arrived home one evening and my mother told me she was going to the school to have a meeting with the nuns about my future. What I didn't realise until many years later was that my older sister, who had achieved incredible results for a girl, with 10 GCEs, was refused the opportunity by my parents to let her stay on at school free to do her A levels with a view to being shortlisted for Oxford. Basically, she was sent out to work to help keep the ever-growing family, while the meagre fees that had been paid for her were now transferred to me. What a poor substitute for the school! My mother came home triumphant and said I had to work hard and I might do well! I didn't know how I could do that since the only thing I was good at was washing dishes and cleaning the house. So there was a lot of fear around going to 'big school'.

A few days before starting at the school I went through an initiation ceremony which involved being sat in the bath with a bowl on my head and my father came and cut round it. I had asked for my hair to be cut so that I could look grown up and also to be rid of the dreaded ringlets. I thought this might involve going to a hairdresser and having a modern cut like my sister. Instead, I had to face my first day at senior school with a bowl cut and a large ribbon on the top. l looked like the ridiculous cartoon character Toots in the *Bunty* comic of the 1960s and, to rub salt in the wound further, the family gave me that very nickname.

Once at school, I managed to make one good friend, who always brought a delicious packed lunch which she shared with me. Her mother eventually put in some special bits just for me. My packed lunch from home consisted every day of a flask of hot water, an Oxo cube and plain white bread without butter. I tried not to get embarrassed in the lunch hall when everyone else who had packed lunch would pull out delicious-looking sandwiches and fruit and occasionally even a piece of chocolate. The other thing I was painfully aware of was that my school uniform was so thin from wear (it had been passed down from sister to sister), you could see the light through it when you held it up. Eventually we darned the gymslip so that it didn't suddenly develop a hole one day when I was at school. The highlight of my 'uniform' was when my mother came by a second-hand boater hat, which was part of the summer uniform. She didn't like the fact that the straw had become so brown from the sun and it looked second hand. After discussion with my father, who was incredibly creative when it came to restorations, he came up with a plan. He disappeared with the hat and two hours later presented back to my mother, a bright, shiny, white hat covered in Pammastic paint. The hat now had the bonus of being completely waterproof as it sported a gloss finish to it! It would have made a fine advert for Dulux Brilliant White paint and no matter how many times I tried to leave it behind on the school bus, like a boomerang it returned to me because no one else had a hat quite like that! It was at times like this that you would run out of ideas of how to 'normalise' such a strange home and I resorted to sinking into silent embarrassment where I hoped the ground would suddenly open up and swallow me. On my last day at school, I left my boater hat on the school gatepost for fear that my mother might put it into the second-hand shop hoping to make some money from it. Necessity might be the mother of invention but in our home, it resulted in some pretty weird inventions. To be fair to my father, a waterproof boater hat for schools might have caught on had it had a more subtle finish to it!

Given the fact that nothing changed at home with regards to my role as 'Cinderella' there was no chance to excel at any of my school work except English, though even this subject held no joy for me. By now I had become so painfully shy that I dreaded the lessons which increasingly consisted of reading out loud. The book was *The Children of the New Forest* which was incredibly tedious and full of difficult words to pronounce. The woman who taught us was a rather large Irish woman whose fat feet bulged out of the sides of her open sandals as she tottered on their rather unfortunate high heels. She would burst into the room, sweep her way to the window and exclaim as if she were about to deliver a Shakespearean speech:

"Open the windows, gals."

I remember watching fascinated by the fat and folds of loose skin at the top of her arms which would wobble as she reached across to ensure that every window was open. It mattered not whether a Siberian wind was blowing outside, the object of the exercise was to make sure that every one of us was still awake at the end of the class. She would then pick on a reader and we would each have a ten-minute spell of taking it in turns to read from our books. I would look at the clock and pray that it would not make it to my turn before the bell went for the next lesson.

Chapter 2 - The Tibetan Monks

I hated the sound of my own voice and dreaded the thought of making a mistake in pronunciation and becoming an object of ridicule by the rest of the class. This fortunately never happened in this class but I lived with fear all the time and my hands were permanently sweaty and trembled as if I was going into battle.

Once in a Latin lesson, my fear was inadvertently relaxed by the sight of two butterflies outside the window chasing each other on the wind currents. They did an exquisite *pas de deux* around each other in my full view and then they separated out and came back for a full passionate tango at the end. I marvelled at their freedom and began thinking how we, who are supposedly more evolved life forms, were here shut in a classroom for hours learning about dead people's ideas, while they, the butterflies, were free to roam the countryside. I then turned inwards on my own thoughts and began to get further lost in the idea of where thoughts went. I started at the end rather than the beginning of 'What is thought?' I knew thought was there so where did it go to if you never expressed it to anyone and what therefore was its purpose? The class were declining the different cases of 'mensa - the table' and, like Churchill before me, I could never understand why you would want to learn the vocative case to say: "Oh table!" But clearly the Romans seemed to think that you did. The lesson droned on with reading from passages about people dressed in togas and which ending a toga should have if it was being described as: "Oh beautiful toga!" Thoughts of fat, debauched Romans and their togas soon tired me and it wasn't long before I drifted out the window again. Suddenly a piece of chalk hit the side of my face with a sting and 'Little Hitler' as he was lovingly known as by the students - a short, stout, balding Irish man with a grey Hitler moustache - shouted at me:

"Stand up!"

I was now to become a creature of ridicule. Sadly, we had moved on during my daydream from togas back to the declension of 'the table' and other words that followed the same declension.

Once I was standing to attention, I was asked first to explain what I had been doing. Still in part trance, I muttered that I was wondering where thoughts went to. This was quite the most hilarious thing that the entire class seemed to have ever heard. Several minutes of ridicule ensued spurred on by Little Hitler and then abruptly ended with him announcing that my thoughts were best served by learning declensions and that, in fact, is what I would be doing after school that day. The star pupil was then selected to stand and decline her table to perfection to the wonderment of the less mentally developed of the class and to the pride of Little Hitler who was able to prove QED that he was indeed a great master of the teaching profession. I sat down again and after that humiliating experience, I decided to tame my trance experiences to very limited sessions. Yet it was to be my ability to not only go into trance but lead others into it that would be one of my careers for the future. Life would be so much better for people and for creativity if we could break outside of boxing and moulding people and look to their innate talents.

If I lived in fear and dread of these lessons, the worst was yet to come. Gymnastics and PE in the hall provided my greatest nightmare – jumping onto the springboard and across the wooden horse. We would stand in a queue waiting to execute this performance and as it got nearer to my turn, my legs would turn to jelly and I would break out in a cold sweat. Inevitably, what I dreaded most was manifested before everybody's eyes. I would land like a sack of potatoes in the middle of the horse, nearly doing myself an injury in the process and then tried to descend from it as if nothing untoward had happened. This was a little difficult as going bright red to the roots of my hair was my pièce de resistance whenever I had done a particularly fine cock up! Of course, I was not the only one that this happened to because not all in the class were destined to become a budding Olga Korbut but when you suffer from non-existent self-esteem you assume automatically that you are the only person that this happens to.

You become so self-absorbed with your own inadequacies to the point of obsession – dwelling on it, manifesting it and feasting on it. Robbing someone of their self-esteem from childhood is, in my opinion, the worst disservice you can do to a person and is incredibly difficult to repair. It frequently results in the person attaching no worth to their life and is one of the prime causes of attracting abusive relationships in adult life along with being undervalued in the work place.

When it wasn't raining, hockey became the outdoor version of this if the pitch wasn't a sea of mud. The optimum time for hockey was considered to be a freezing cold frosty morning when the clods of earth were solid on the ground and the studs of the boots had some sort of grip. Dressed in short games skirts and short sleeved t-shirts, out we went to be toughened up by doing battle with the elements and chasing a rock of a ball up and down trying to get it between two goal posts. I tried where possible to get any position but the confrontational bully-off where you were likely to get the shins whopped off you either by a hockey stick or the rock ball. After about three lessons, I could not tolerate

Chapter 2 - The Tibetan Monks

'games lessons' anymore and so more often than not I would go to the toilet in the changing room and wait until everyone had left. I then made for the school library and hid behind the high bookshelves and sat cross-legged on the floor. It was on one such occasion that I lifted a large encyclopaedia down from the bottom shelf and became engrossed in it. As I was turning the pages, I came across a picture of several monks dressed in orange robes sitting in the cold mountain snows of Tibet. They had towels wrapped around their shoulders and the scene caught my attention. As I read on, it explained that cold wet towels had been placed on their shoulders to demonstrate how they were able to elevate their body temperatures to such an extent that steam would rise from the towels as they dried them in the cold of the mountain air. It was thought to be done by 'mind power' and they would practise a form of 'meditation'. I do not know why I was so absorbed with this story and the picture but I still see it today in my inner world as clearly as I saw it in the picture that day in the library. I wondered at having such a mind that could alter your own body temperature. If you could do that, what else might you do with your mind? At that point the bell went and I could see my class returning from the netball court, which I could see from the large library windows. I managed to keep up my truancy for a term until the end of term report had to be written and the teacher stated very clearly that she did not know this student as she had not attended any games lessons at all! This ended my retreat to the library and truancy no longer became an option as I was now well and truly on the watch list. But once again, spirit had crept into my life and planted the seeds. I never forgot my monks in the Himalayas and, apart from dance, this was now the only other ambition I had in life ... to find out how they trained their minds to this level. It would take nearly a lifetime and a serious illness before I would fulfil this ambition and I would be shown much more than how to raise my body temperature!

By the end of year two, I was seriously behind with my work. I did no homework because as soon as I was home it was my job to help with my younger brother and sister and prepare supper for 'Daddy'. It was never questioned much as to why I got below average marks and at home although I was chastised for wasting good money it was also partly expected and explained by my mother's phrase:

"You can't make a silk purse out of a sow's ear!"

Home life and school life became unbearable. I began to get acutely depressed and when a new young creative nun arrived at the school and

asked us in the Religious Education lesson to write an essay about our hopes and dreams for the future, I wrote one line:
"I don't have any hopes and dreams for the future. I just want to die."
Safeguarding in schools was not part of the norm in those days but she quickly took the 'essay' to Rev. Mother and I was asked to go to her office. I was told to sit down and she was very kind, asking me what could be done to help the situation. She asked if I would like to be a boarder and I said I would love it but there was no money to pay. She said she would see what could be done for the next term. I do not know how the situation was explained to my mother but clearly they kept our talk and my essay confidential and the next term I became a boarder. It was heaven. It mattered not that I had only two homemade skirts and sweaters to wear when all the other girls had a full wardrobe. There was camaraderie among the boarders and a definite segregation from the day girls. The only difficulty was weekends and eventually I made a new good friend among the boarders who knew what my home was about and invited me back for weekends to their family home. I was so happy and I went from second from the bottom in the class to sixth from the top in one term and was given a special prize at the end of term for 'effort'. Life was good and although I felt I had betrayed my parents by telling the truth, it was a lesson I was to carry through life: how will things ever change if you don't tell the truth? I did well at school up until the time of my GCEs and was given a grant to stay at school to study A levels. As I began my first year of A levels studying Botany, Zoology and Chemistry, life circumstances took over. But, once again at the time I did not know that what I would learn from this would be more important than any exams I was studying for.

My mother became ill and with my younger sister and brother to be looked after, I was summoned home. It was almost impossible to sustain studying, travelling to school by bus and looking after my siblings and my father. My mother's illness turned out to be breast cancer – on the left side. In my own recent studies on breast cancer, I have come across some interesting psychological and emotional studies that show the left side to be connected with mother and prominent female figures in your life and the right is connected with father and significant males. My mother never felt mothered once her own mother died when she was 12 years old. In addition, prior to my mother's illness, she had suffered several family bereavements. Her younger brother had died unexpectedly from a heart condition and at the same time she was also expecting a telegram any day to say that her younger sister had died. She too had

Chapter 2 - The Tibetan Monks

breast cancer. Her brother dying was a complete shock as she had been very close to him. We had become estranged from her younger sister and their family due to a family feud and the only memory of Auntie Julia that I have is her being carried by my father from a car park across the road from our house and laid like a small child on the settee. She was approximately 6 stone at the time and she already looked like a corpse. Later, I overheard my mother saying to my father, "they have taken every organ out of her body". What I learnt eventually, was that extensive surgery had been carried out and even part of her pituitary gland had been removed to try to stop the cancer from spreading. Chemotherapy was not offered to her at this time, only surgery and radiotherapy, and clearly nothing was having any effect. She died shortly after the visit to our home but at least the two sisters had had time to make their peace. Naturally, my mother was filled with dread when she discovered she too had the same illness. Her GP had tried to reassure her by declaring that he had yet to see a malignant lump in that place but the surgeon soon proved otherwise. My mother had a left-sided radical mastectomy with several underarm lymph nodes removed and this was accompanied by arm swelling and inability to raise her arm above her head to even brush her hair on that side. Although it was horrifying for me as a young teenage girl watching my mother in this state, I am grateful now that I witnessed it and I remember thinking to myself at the time:

'If this ever happens to me, I will never have this treatment.'

It was as much the debilitating psychological effects on her as the physical. Her coping mechanism became depression, not talking about feelings and finally dousing them in alcohol. She eventually became incapable of tears as she tried to balance a lopsided body in a dress when going out for an evening out. The prosthesis was completely gross and did not stay inside the pocketed bra provided so it was not unusual for it to become completely dislodged and at times even finish up on the floor in front of her because of the weight. In the end, the only way she could attempt to balance it was to have this heavy gel blob strapped into an all-in-one corset no matter what the weather so that it stayed in place. That coupled with the large scar left across her breast made me even more convinced that this type of mutilation would never be for me. Reconstruction surgery was not offered and it was considered that mutilation was a small price to pay for your life. Years later, when I had made a very different decision from the one my mother had, my oldest sister tried to say that things had come a long way over the past fifty years. I am, however, unable to see that - since cutting, burning and poisoning are still the procedure when it comes to conventional therapy. Billions of dollars have been spent and soon nearly as many people will have been 'treated' in what feels like for me one of the largest experiments ever conducted. Nowadays, the poisoning seems to be more in vogue as the pharmaceutical companies are bigger business than radiotherapy, even though cancer stem cells are not destroyed by chemotherapy and the immune system is left shot to pieces when they come back with a vengeance after the five-year survival prognosis. This would appear to be supported by a small article entitled 'Cancerous cells "turn cannibal" to feed tumours' that was published on 19th September 2019 by the *Metro* newspaper. Scientists at Tulane University School of Medicine in New Orleans found that 'cannibal' cancer cells consume nearby cells so they can regrow after chemotherapy. Chemotherapy targets the DNA of a cancer cell, which usually kills it, but breast cancer cells with a gene TP53 are only stunned by it and therefore it lies dormant. These cells then effectively 'eat' and digest others, giving them the nutrition they require to regrow once again into a tumour. They were also aware that some lung and bone cancers do the same. When many years later I received my diagnosis, it was not the fear that I might die but the pictures of my mother's battle with cancer that flashed through my mind. The very idea of mastectomy, which was my surgical option, made me feel physically sick and frozen with fear. It seems unbelievable that I had worked in the past as a nurse and now I heave when even going to visit someone in a hospital.

Following the surgery, my mother was sent for radiotherapy. Radiotherapy was in its infancy then, as was the discovery of tamoxifen, a drug which she would also be given later on in her treatment. I am sure if you could have measured the radiation emitted from her it would have been off the Geiger counter as clinical trials were just beginning at that time to monitor survival rates for those with or without radiotherapy. The doses administered were clearly experimental, hence the clinical trials. On her return from a one particularly long day, as she was first to have been picked up by hospital transport and the last to be dropped back, I recall her coming home and coughing up large amounts of black fluid. She would say to me that she felt the dose was too much as if her lungs were being burnt. It terrified me further seeing all the blue line markings around the area where once her breast had been and where the radiotherapy was to be targeted and how she was not allowed to take a bath. This was something my mother could not bear and we found a

Chapter 2 - The Tibetan Monks

way to make a shallow bath and I would wash her carefully avoiding the area for irradiation.

During this time with my mother, I started to understand her a little more. She once described to me an occasion when her Uncle Connor had arrived back from the Missions. This was referring to a time when priests were sent abroad to what would have been named the Congo in Africa. His job was to convert black African children into Christianity. Periodically, he would come back to Ireland for a holiday and, unfortunately, he arrived at a time when my mother had finished her schooling and was about to embark on a career in England. The career was that of a 'dispensing chemist', nowadays known as a pharmacist, and she had secured a place at Boots in Nottingham. My mother was a bright, intelligent woman truly gifted in mathematics and science and it is hardly surprising that the genes came out in my older sister and my older son. She needed £10 to start her training and she was waiting for the money to be sent from another uncle in America. No sooner did Uncle Con hear what she was going off to do, he warned her father about the evils of what she would be doing: namely, selling illicit medicine over the counter. By this he meant the contraceptive pill, illegal in Southern Ireland and banned by the Catholic Church. Her father watched for the envelope to come from America, commandeered the money and that was to be the end of my mother's career. In the end, she took herself back to England to work in an ammunitions factory as a wages clerk. Before leaving, she had met my father who was working in a draper's shop in the nearest village. Interestingly it was my mother's love of knitting that took her to the shop looking for new patterns so once again her skills have been passed on. Eventually she found a better job on the railways as a booking clerk and there she amazed her colleagues with her skills of addition when it came to long queues of passengers asking for tickets all around the country. She would add everything in her head and her till at the end of her shift always balanced. The senior staff asked her to devise an addition chart on the wall to assist her colleagues in finding a quick way to add the cost of tickets on a busy Monday morning. How frustrating she must have found life! She should have become a career woman instead of a baby-making factory. Had she thought about it more deeply when initially coming to England, she may again have found more opportunities but sometimes if a dream is crushed, we make different choices - carpe diem or the moment is lost. It is choices, right or wrong, that can alter our lives completely. A thought crossed my mind at that moment - was her cancer in some way connected with her inability to fulfil her career as a pharmacist? Do your emotions dictate what happens to your body?

My life now would take a very different direction. My school years had ended and I barely scraped two A levels. I left school supposedly ready for the outside world. Added to my jigsaw were even more pieces: a struggle with low self-esteem and depression; the role of telling the truth; breast cancer and its treatment; caring for someone with ill health; and dealing with that person's use of alcohol as a coping mechanism. Along with all of this, spirit had nudged its way in again and now presented me with Tibetan monks, training of the mind and meditation. Again, what I was to do with these pieces I had no idea nor did I even spend much time contemplating them, for the world of work was awaiting me.

CHAPTER 3

Into the Outside World

My first introduction to the working world was that of office life. I began at the Automobile Association and my job was to sort cheques and postal orders for either new or renewal subscriptions. There was also of course a tray for complaints. The staff were all women with the exception of the male boss. We sat in rows of approximately eight people long and six people deep. Our boss faced us so that if we had any queries, we could put our hand up and either go up or he would come and address the issue with us at our desk. It appeared to me even more suffocating than school and if you needed to use the toilet you put your hand up and were given permission for 10 minutes. If you went over this time a colleague was sent to investigate why you were gone so long. Sadly this situation for women has not changed a great deal. They are still in low paid, part-time jobs, particularly if they have children. The issue of equal pay for women is nicely got around by making it a job done by women so that there can be no equalising it with a man's pay because he is usually the boss. The alternative is to make it a taboo subject in society to talk about salaries. I knew that I would not be able to manage this job for very long so when my sister suggested nursing, I seriously considered it. After all, I had practically nursed my mother through cancer. My sister had wanted to be a nurse since watching the romantic series on TV of *Dr Kildare* and she liked the idea of a uniform, but that was about the extent of her desire to be a nurse. I started to apply and was accepted in both London and Dorset and since I was a country girl at heart, I chose the latter option, particularly as it was close to the sea. On my first day I met Annette, who was to become my lifelong friend. Sadly, she too has developed breast cancer even though there was no family history and she has bravely gone through all the conventional therapy. I also developed a friendship with Brenda and we had long discussions into the night on spirituality and philosophy. She was a few years older and I thrived on her knowledge and flow of books, particularly those of Herman Hesse, which, with my limited home background, I had no idea existed. The world of Siddhartha and his path to enlightenment by becoming one with the river and the ferryman touched me deeply and this was enhanced further by the song by Ralph McTell entitled 'The Ferryman'. The analogy of the river was to present itself again during my treatment, when by that time I had long since buried all this part of my life. As I underwent acupuncture as part of my treatment, I rediscovered it with much more meaning the second time around. This period when I was training to be a nurse was such a wonderful time, I felt as though I was coming to life and a flame was growing within me. I was with a like-minded person and we could bounce ideas off each other. There was also so much meaningful music being produced in the seventies. In the evenings when I finished work, I immersed myself in the music of Tom Paxton, Cat Stevens, John Denver, Simon & Garfunkel and of course Joan Baez. Whenever I could, I attended concerts and experienced being in the powerful group energy that is found when souls unite. I had a guitar and taught myself to play and I recognised what a powerful tool music is for healing. It allowed me to release much of the emotional trauma of childhood. It touches the essence of people no matter what country or culture they are from as it knows no boundaries.

Nursing was not really for me but it was such a relief to have accommodation away from home and my shattered confidence slowly returned. However, three years after training, I felt that I was a worse nurse than when I first began. This was mainly because the care of patients was so rushed and there never seemed to be time to talk to them for very long. I realised that psychological care was as important, if not more so, for a patient's recovery and this seemed to be sadly lacking in the hospital environment. I don't feel much has changed as the work pressure for nurses increases. Following my training, I took a staff nurse's role for almost a year, taking care of acute admissions in the elderly care ward. It was a good experience and I worked with many lovely Caribbean staff, but by now I was looking for something more. Interestingly, the thing that I remember most from that placement was sharing a house with a Japanese nurse who disappeared off every weekend. We got talking one evening and she told me she would be leaving shortly to stay

Chapter 3 - Into the Outside World

in an Ashram. It is never a coincidence the people that you meet in life, and here, once again, I was being nudged in a direction that was one that would have been a good idea to explore. But bound by convention, how would I explain to my family that I was giving up a good career and heading for an Ashram! Leaving home had given me the opportunity to explore all sorts of interests including yoga. I found a class which also involved meditation. Here we were encouraged to take our minds to higher realms and in the first session I took myself out of body so that I was looking down on the room and watching everyone in Shavasana pose lying on the floor. I then took myself higher to looking down on the earth. I could see the blue colour of the oceans as if viewing it from space. I felt no fear, partly because I was in a group and partly because I knew now I was among people who meditated and it was normal to mind travel.

It was only a matter of time before I started exploring other religions and ways of life, and the belief in past lives in Hinduism and Buddhism particularly fascinated me. I constantly questioned why we were given 'mind'. There had to be something more to mind than just thinking about daily routines and inventing more physical things. Always there was the burning question:

"Is there something more than just this physical world?"

It was on one of my weekend visits to my parents that I spotted in TV listings in the newspaper, a television programme called the *Bloxham Tapes* presented by Magnus Magnusson, a popular Icelandic journalist and TV presenter known for the programme *Mastermind*. My parents at this late hour were heading for bed and my father couldn't understand what was so special about a programme that warranted staying up until gone midnight. Reluctantly, I told him what I was going to watch and waited for the onslaught of ridicule. I was not to be disappointed and he expressed his usual distaste for anything that did not fit in with his thinking. His customary repertoire covered it nicely: "What a load of old bunkum! Anyone can make up this load of old baloney." In his voice was the typical scorn, exasperation and disappointment that I was taking an avid interest in this kind of sorcery but I stood my ground and they went to bed. It was an hour-long programme that explored the works of the hypnotherapist Arnold Bloxham, who had recorded regressions into previous lives. Perhaps the most fascinating one was that of a subject who was regressed back to the time of the Jewish massacres in York in 1190. She called herself Rebecca at that time. Little was known of this history but Professor Dobson had published a paper on it. Rebecca had described under hypnosis the crypt of a church that she had taken shelter in with her child to try to avoid death. Eventually she was caught and murdered. At the time the programme was being made, one of the churches in St Mary's at Castlegate in York was undergoing conversion into a museum and the workmen found below the church a crypt very similar to that described by Rebecca. I watched the programme with a rising sense of excitement – so was this true that there really was such a thing as past lives? I was 18 years old and I suddenly had an overpowering feeling that one day I would study hypnotherapy.

Over the months, I was becoming restless and I had hitchhiked my way around Europe with various nursing friends and had the real travel bug. I also attended my sister's wedding in Canada and hiked and camped with my cousins. One of my cousins was training as an occupational therapist and this sounded more creative than my nursing career so I applied and was accepted in Exeter. I enjoyed the training, which included anatomy, particularly learning all the muscles of the body, psychology and many different crafts. The craft that most interested me was weaving and having made a good friend, we then house shared. We found evening classes in spinning and both of us acquired an Ashford spinning wheel and investigated how to do natural dying. My love of working with yarns and colours was being reawakened so, not surprisingly, at the end of our training, my friend headed for the Shetland Islands to be a tweed weaver on the Harris looms and I went to Mullingar in Ireland and became a hand weaver. At last, I had found a job I thoroughly enjoyed. Even though there were days that I wove similar scarves, shawls and table mats for our craft store, some for export and some for the larger Dublin stores, I never felt that the days were long and heavy. Each day was a joy to go to work and there was something very mesmerising about the sound of the shuttle going to and fro making a lub-dub noise as it hit against the shuttle box.

Unfortunately, you never quite get it all in life. On the home front, I shared with two sisters who were not particularly happy to share their house with an outsider, and from England too. The accommodation had been very kindly found by my employer and since the salary as a hand weaver was so low, I could not afford to stay anywhere else. As compensation, I was given shares in the company for as long as I was part of it. By my second year in Ireland, Bobby Sands, a provisional member of the IRA was starving himself to death in the Maze prison. When he died, black flags were hung out of the windows of many of the houses in Mullingar and it became obvious how many supporters were

Chapter 3 - Into the Outside World

living there. One of my close friends had been living in the town for many years and considered herself Irish because one of her parents was Irish (the other was English) and lived in the countryside not far from her. She had bought a house, had started her own hairdressing business and got on very well with the locals. They had considered her one of them. However, once Bobby Sands died, she was boycotted for several weeks and without her business she had no money to pay her mortgage. She decided it was time to sell up and move West. I too felt uncomfortable and once again out of place. I also felt somewhat guilty that I was not using my medical trainings and that, since it was time to move on, maybe I should reconsider a career back in one of these fields. I had no desire to move back to England, nor to my family. My father in particular was very pleased I had returned to the 'Auld country' and was perhaps looking forward to the time when he would eventually retire from business, go back to Ireland and have a family member close by. He had even considered loaning me the money to buy a house in Ireland at one stage, but thankfully this didn't happen and I was now free to move on.

It was at this time I began to get very low mentally and couldn't see a way out of the situation. I returned to my old negative patterns of behaviour from my school years and struggled with suicidal thoughts. Childhood abuse never leaves you until you can learn to love yourself and this was to take many more years to achieve. In my young twenties, I had no idea that the love has to come from within you first. Only when you have love and respect for yourself will you automatically attract this from others. I felt alone and desperate and was beginning to give up when an Irish newspaper came my way with an advert for an occupational therapy post with VSO in Bangladesh. Here again was a voice from the past. In 1971 when I was 17, Joan Baez did a concert for the flood victims of Bangladesh and the news showed constant pictures of starving children in the flood-affected areas. I remember saying to my mother that one day I would go there to work and she begged me not to as she considered it to be the same 'white man's grave' that the Congo had proved to be for so many missionaries. It makes me really wonder about how much of our lives are predestined. I had known that one day I would go there and now, just when I was at my lowest ebb, here was an advert. I applied and was accepted. The most difficult part was telling my employer as not only would I be leaving but his daughter, who was also the other main weaver, had announced that she was pregnant.

My mother was shocked at my decision and I heard later from my brother that they had no idea I was becoming a missionary and hadn't seen any signs of it coming on! Clearly, it was another sign to them of my instability and the likelihood of my settling down was becoming more remote by the day. It all happened very swiftly and within a matter of weeks I was in London for training. I was the only female in a group of five going to Bangladesh and we were the only ones, out of a much larger team of volunteers being sent to other parts of the globe, who were given the free book entitled *Where There is No Doctor*. I didn't care, I needed to feel useful and have a purpose in life and I didn't feel I had either, neither in Ireland nor England.

On the morning I was to fly, my father was taken ill with acute abdominal pain and I didn't know whether to stay or leave but both parents begged me to go with the group or it might be difficult to settle in later. I left reluctantly as I was worried what impact this might have on my mother. Five years post treatment for left breast cancer she had received the all clear and so her monitoring had been reduced. However, she was not to remain all clear for very long and she found the second lump in her right breast which again resulted in a mastectomy and radiotherapy. I had been living in Ireland at the time and it was a long time before she told me about it. I was shocked and upset that she had not thought to tell me and also that it had returned. It was my brother who made the link that her ill health coincided with each time one of us left home. It was as if my mother felt her role was over once her children flew the nest and knowing what I know now, depression would have quickly set in without a purpose to her life. My father was eventually diagnosed with gall stones and had his gall bladder swiftly removed and the news was relayed to me in Dhaka. Knowing that he was making a recovery, I felt relieved and free to get on with my life. It was to be very different from anything I had ever known.

On the flight over, the plane had had to stop in Calcutta because of engine problems so we stopped the night at a hotel courtesy of British Airways and had the chance to wander around for the evening. One of my travel companions had already done a stint in Sri Lanka so was happy to accompany me around the streets. I felt as if I had walked in on a film set. Nothing prepared me for the smell, the poverty, the colours and the laughter of the people I was watching, and the sheer noise levels of life in the East was something else again. I marvelled at the lengths they went to recycle everything. The women would roll buffalo and cow dung in their hands and slap it on the outside of the walls of their houses to dry

Chapter 3 – Into the Outside World

into cakes in the warm sunshine. This was their fuel supply to cook their evening food. All around me were adverts for computers and yet there were people scrabbling around rubbish tips dressed in rags and looking for things to recycle. It was like East meets West gone mad!

The following day we flew on to Dhaka and were met by Jim, our VSO project manager. He calmly explained to us that there had been a military coup overnight and General Ershad was now in power and tanks were trundling down the main street of Dhanmondi in Dhaka. He looked at me especially, for a reaction, and said that if anyone wanted to go home now, he could arrange for our flight back. Jim later revealed that he had a preconceived idea of me having read my qualifications and the fact that I had been educated at a convent boarding school. He decided I would be naive and spoilt. He was not wrong about the former but the latter definitely didn't apply. My mother had paid two shillings and six pence a week for my education and, from a very young age, I had been trained how to get money out of a sealed charity box which sat on the top of the dreaded electricity cupboard at the bottom of the stairs. It probably went to fund the likes of Uncle Con on his missionary stints in the Congo. As a child I was taught how to insert a knife in the coin slot, turn the box upside down and shake it until the coins slid down the knife and dropped onto the table, I would then do a count up. This was a weekly event on Fridays when my mother needed to buy fish for the family and my father's wages had run out. She then lived in fear in case someone from the church arrived to collect the box, which usually coincided with when it was empty, which was more often than not! She would then ask them to call back having done the rounds of our toy money boxes. As long as a few coins rattled in it she could save face at the door.

Jim was afraid I might be put off by my accommodation, which left a lot to be desired, so he had arranged for me to stay for a few days with a couple whose husband was working for Save the Children. My first introduction was meeting Lauren, who was standing on the flat roof of their large rented house and, as we watched the tanks go by, she was getting more and more excited by the prospect that they may be airlifted home. She had hated her Bangladesh experience and would have been more than happy to see it cut short. With three young children, I think she had had enough of her husband's charitable activities.

Things did eventually settle down and I moved to my new accommodation having been temporarily accommodated at Jim's house after Lauren's. Clearly, he was excited at the prospect of a new young female in the country, and from a convent too, and he wasted no time in trying to take advantage even though he clearly was living with another female project leader who was away when I arrived. My accommodation was indeed as awful as Jim had described it, but it was better than the option of living in the house I now found myself in and so I insisted on a rapid move. My own accommodation was not only a basic Bangladeshi house but I was also sharing the bathroom with three paralysed boys so my job was to clean it before I could wash. After some time, I got to know the expat community and, as they left to go home for long periods of time both summer and winter, I had a permanent job house sitting. As one family returned from leave, the next one was ready to go, so I moved to many different beautiful houses every few months. This meant I had the luxury of air conditioning after a day's work. The servants also came with the house and once they realised I was not a rich foreigner like their master, they bought cheaply from the market and served me the most delicious meals. So I had the best of both worlds, luxury by night and volunteering by day. I realised how bizarre my life was when the social worker and I went to the slum area of Dhanmondi to rescue a paralysed lady from the flood waters. Just as I had seen on the television when I was 17, here I now was wading through the flood waters up to my thighs. It was a particularly heavy monsoon and the rivers had broken their banks causing many of the streets of Dhaka to flood. The children were delighted and had their nets at the ready to catch some fish. I rescued the Singer sewing machine, which was how she made a living once her husband had walked out on her when she had become paralysed following childbirth. She was lifted onto the rickshaw along with her sewing machine and brought to the Centre for the Rehabilitation of the Paralysed to be taken care of until the flood water subsided. That evening I was invited by one of the expats to the Swedish Embassy for supper. I was referred to as Memsahib and served sparkling wine from a silver tray. I wondered what the waiter might have thought if he had known where I had been for the day. I never discussed much about my work. I think the expat community thought it was very noble if a little nuts. I felt fortunate to have seen the country through many different communities and I did start to question western development in these countries. The Americans were doing a rural electrification project bringing electricity to the villages. This might have seemed a good idea but what in fact happened was that instead of by night the village people going to sleep, they now had lighting, which filled their huts with mosquitoes. Really what would have been more useful was clean

Chapter 3 – Into the Outside World

drinking water. Diarrhoeal diseases would have been reduced and, with it, infant mortality. If mothers then realised that their child would survive beyond the age of one, it would have been easier to introduce contraception and reduce the population by contraception rather than death. The other aspect of western technology was it brought knowledge of the western life style and it was not long before even the beautiful jungle areas of Jalchatra had *Dallas* ringing out from the one television set in the village. They would look at me and ask me if this was the way people lived in the West as they watched men and women jumping in and out of bed, cheating on each other with different partners. What could I really answer? It was what it was! In spite of the television, I enjoyed my occasional weekend invites into the jungle. A young American nun had befriended me through one of the expat communities and whenever she was making a trip, she would invite me. The nuns lived very well with access to American goods from the go-downs as they were called – warehouses holding American goods so that the expats didn't go short while living in underdeveloped countries. This even ran to the occasional bottle of wine and chocolates!

Close by in the jungle area were two villages, one Muslim and one Christian, and the difference in poverty levels between the females in particular was obvious. In the Christian village, the women worked on projects for Oxfam and had their goods marketed through the shops – embroidery, particularly cushion covers and wall hangings and charming greetings cards with pictures made from gold straw. Consequently, these women had beautiful saris and were much more outgoing. This was not the case in the Muslim village and rumour had it that some women shared a sari so only the newest wife got to come out of the hut. In Dhaka too, once the women had served their purpose they were thrown onto the streets with their female children and left to fend for themselves. Here again was my theme being replayed of the rejection of women and the female child. Save the Children and Oxfam helped to fund a project in Dhaka similar to that of the women in the village and they could live in the house where the project was run from. It wasn't long before the men realised that they were earning a living and so began stoning the windows of the house and jeering outside. Being in these environments makes one seriously consider whether it is right to impose our form of democracy if the people themselves are not ready for it because if they were, they would bring it about themselves. Women in western countries even today have still settled to be second class citizens and little has changed by us getting the vote. Domestic abuse and financial and sexual exploitation are rampant. So how would these women fare if when given the opportunity for financial independence it resulted in their lives being endangered because of it? One day, women collectively throughout the world must reach a stage where they decide the suppression has gone on long enough and unite for the greater good of themselves and their societies.

My life in Bangladesh was an eye opener but it looked as though it was to come to an end after six months. I had arrived on a tourist visa with the idea of converting it to a proper long-term working visa once I was there. However, the project I was working for was deemed politically hot and the girl who ran it was from the UK but had no visa at all thanks to an argument with higher officials when she had 'kidnapped' the patients from the top floor of a state hospital where they had been left to die. In Bangladesh, paralysis was thought to be catching and if your family members were too frightened to care for you and you could not pay a large baksheesh to a carer, then you were left to die and preferably out of sight. Hence the choice of the top floor for their existence. So as my boss had permission to neither stay nor leave, I too was in the same boat. Eventually, through my Irish parents I was able to be a dual national. I could stay as an Irish citizen without a visa for a considerable length of time because Ireland was one of the first countries to recognise Bangladesh as a free independent country after the war with what is now Pakistan. It was on the trip to leave Bangladesh as a British citizen and re-enter as an Irish one that I met my future husband.

One of my lasting memories of Bangladesh was a rainy monsoon night coming back in a rickshaw from an evening out with friends. I was in my rubber flip-flops and there was an electrical storm going on. I jumped down from the rickshaw, paid my money and he cycled off into the night. I went to open the metal gate at the bottom of the drive and received a powerful electric shock from the gate. For what seemed like several seconds I could not pull myself away from it and with great difficulty I eventually did and shouted at the chokidar who was in the gatehouse at the top of the drive. He walked down in the rain and let me in. I tried to explain about the shock I had experienced from the gate but he didn't appear to really understand what I was saying. It wasn't until I chatted with one of my American friends from the rural electrification programme a few days later that I realised how lucky I was to be alive. It is also interesting that many years later I recalled this event with a shaman acquaintance who informed me that long ago this was

Chapter 3 – Into the Outside World

one of the initiation rites of passage for a shaman. I am not so sure about that but I do wonder if it somehow increased my vibrational levels.

I had the opportunity to stay on in Bangladesh but by this time my future husband was waiting for me to finish my contract. I had already delayed because a royal visit had taken place to the centre and I then needed to hand over to my new volunteer. I left for England way over the baggage allowance as I had been given a large painted wooden box and an abundance of gifts so that my Bengali brothers and sisters would not be forgotten when I was far away. It was sad leaving it all behind. I had learnt about caring and love for each other in this supposedly poverty-stricken land. On return to England, the culture shock seemed to be worse for me coming back. As I sat on the underground train with everyone avoiding eye contact and saw miserable faces as people trudged their way to work, I wondered if I could ever return to England to live.

I went back once more to the East, this time to India. My fiancé and I were married in the Catholic Church as the priest was the only one who would allow us to marry across cultures. It was a beautiful, warm spring day and I had chosen my birthday – 18th March – as my wedding day. I wanted to finally make this day special, a day of happiness, and I thought at last I had found someone who would love me. It was a small wedding, neither my husband's parents (who did not agree with our marriage) nor mine attended. My close friend, Annette, from my nursing days, had flown out specially for the occasion and stayed for a further two-week holiday.

The first two years of our married life, living in India, were really happy and there were no tell-tale signs to indicate that anything would change. India was like a spiritual oasis for me and I had an ideal guide who understood the language, the culture and was also adventurous and caring. During these years, we travelled everywhere by motorbike. We began by visiting the Ellora and Ajanta caves in Maharashtra with their ancient rock temples and paintings. Next, we saw the amazing Dilwara Jain temples of Mount Abu carved in pure white marble as a celebration to the Divine. This exquisite stone would have been taken to the area at a time when the only transport would have been elephants and there was no town close by. Finally, I had a glimpse for my future knowledge of the carvings at Khajuraho, referred to as the Temple of Love. These are actually depictions of kundalini energy but I had little understanding then of what I was being shown and neither did my husband. This ancient world was compelling and absorbing. I was being given a new spiritual insight into something that could only be expressed in exquisite art form and could have only come about as a deep connection through meditation.

We could have remained in India but the discussion of starting a family had arisen. This also brought into consideration the danger of having a child in India with no adequate medical care. I had also thought carefully about the implications of cutting off the West with regards to education. If my children were educated in India then the likelihood of them being able to easily live outside of the country would be slim. After two years of living together in India, we arrived in England on a freezing cold April morning with the snow coming down thick and fast having left a temperature of 37 degrees Celsius in India. The house we were sharing had students in and they did not want to pay for heating so I quickly landed a job as a private nurse working for an agency in London. I had gone from the ridiculous to the sublime – from witnessing abject poverty to wealth like I had never seen before in St John's Wood, Knightsbridge and Kensington. I saw £250 per day spent on a delivery of fresh flowers, presumably ordered by the person who had power of attorney for the patient I was caring for. The patient did not even know where she was, let alone that flowers had been delivered. Naturally I couldn't stop thinking about how many mouths that would have fed back in Bangladesh. After six months of nursing, I decided that permanent night duty, however well it paid, was not conducive to married life. So I trained by day in touch typing, applied for a job as a medical secretary and landed a job in Harley Street.

It was here I met Trish, a truly fascinating woman and we soon became the best of friends. She was to lead me into the world of workshops with a transpersonal psychologist called Ruth White. Trish and I attended regular workshops where we discovered Jungian psychology, meditation, power animals, shamanism and so much more. I was again thrust back into what I had blocked as a child. The visuals I received in meditation were rich and profound and I began at long last to learn what they meant and to understand them. In one such exercise, we were invited to find our power animals, perhaps in a cave, or the water or a forest. What Ruth forgot to say was the words 'or in the air'. I spent a long time searching for my animal and couldn't find one. Just as we were about to be brought out of our meditation an inner voice began:

"*Your animal is not in a cave, or a wood or the water but look up, it is in the air.*"

There above me, in my inner world, soaring into the air was an eagle.

Chapter 3 - Into the Outside World

Once out of meditation, the group members began to describe their animals - bears, snakes, monkeys, wolves. I waited until last as I was feeling embarrassed and uncomfortable. Why was my animal so different? Finally, it was my turn and I explained I had seen an eagle. Both Ruth and Grace, an older wise woman who was assisting in the workshop, stated that it was a very powerful totem animal and generally was at the top of the totem pole in the North American Indian culture. It represented Spirit. On one of our final workshops, we did a meditation and were asked to be shown what gifts the world had given us. Mine was a bird who couldn't fly - it had a broken wing and, as I watched, it was given the whole sky and it started to fly. This reminded me of the broken child who had lain on the floor on so many occasions when I was young. The second gift was a gift to give to a friend. I received Pan - half man, half beast. I later found a little figurine and gave it to Trish as she was like a nymph from another world leading me into this world of magic. The final gift was that of what you had to give to the world. I entered a cave and there was a wall full of cave paintings. The one that stood out the most was a man dressed in a bear skin with strange symbols around him. Following this meditation, I knew that I had received very different messages in the form of rather strange codes, the significance of which I was not completely sure of. I was considering at this time taking a course in hypnotherapy because the *Bloxham Tapes* were a recurrent theme in my thoughts. Maybe this was what the cave paintings were about - that I would help people unlock and unblock their pasts. I was unaware at that time that cave paintings are not about simple daily hunting life telling the story of the daily lives of people in those times. They are in fact about shamanic journeys but I was clearly not ready for this piece of information. All this amazing exploration was happening in my life in 1990. I was discovering the chakras and their colours, meditation and inner journey work and, above all, I was working with the elements of fire, earth, air and water and touched on information regarding alchemy.

With my spirit now burning brightly an opportunity arose to train in reiki I and II with an extremely spiritual woman, Tanmaya Honervogt, a world-renowned healer with deep connections to India. She had such a soft, gentle energy and moved with an almost ethereal, fairy-like quality. Spending a weekend in such energies and living and working in wooden buildings surrounded by trees was truly enchanting. I was reintroduced to music as a form of healing - this time in the form of Sanskrit mantras using the music of Deva Premal and Miten. Their music completely touches the soul like no other. During my training I started to learn more about energy flow and I could feel it in my hands. I had always thought of my hands as being big and ugly as I had to buy men's gloves in order to get them to fit. They had also been used to carry breeze blocks when I was younger and I was praised for how I could carry things like a man! I didn't want to be a man, I had wanted to be a female dancer. However, now I began to appreciate these hands as my perception of them changed. I would feel energy building up in them as they tingled and I practised how far away I could hold them and still feel the tingling. The reiki attunements took me to new vibrational levels and I noticed my eyes had a glow to them as if I had touched another world. I reached a point where I would know intuitively when the reiki treatment was finished for someone as I would have a visual image of their energy flowing like a gushing waterfall from the top of their head to the end of their toes. I would be given visuals of what had been happening in their lives and traumas they had experienced. Life was again wonderful and I felt I was being initiated into a world in which I belonged. In the workshops, although not many people could 'see' what was causing this difference in how people were relating to each other in loving kindness, you could certainly feel it. Unfortunately, when I came away from my weekends there was no one to really practise these skills on and no place to actually work. Gradually over time, like my five positions of ballet had become just a memory, the same was to be true of the magical weekends, the sacred symbols I had learnt and how to feel energy in my hands. I bought a CD of self-healing and also some Premal & Miten music. I hoped that one day, life might afford me the opportunity to use these wonderful new-found talents but for now I was to leave this all behind me, store the contents of my workshops in a small wooden box and enter into the world of motherhood.

My bright, lovely inner world was to shut its door for a very long time and it was to be the summer of 2017 before I would again open the box and out would come pictures from the meditations at that time. Astonishingly, on the aged papers were symbolic drawings of infinity, light and molecules and I felt a shiver pass through my body as I read what I had channelled at that time:

"*I am my own individual self with my given talents.*"
"*You are your own individual self with your talents.*"
"*As long as we offer them to the future with honesty and truth then we have done what we were sent to do.*"

Chapter 3 - Into the Outside World

I had also been given the sound 'Aah' which I had written on the paper. I now know that this is a sacred sound connected with the heart, the fire element and spirit. It is found in God and Goddess names such as Tara and Buddha and is as important and powerful as 'Om'. I had been given all the necessary information for a future time.

CHAPTER 4

Growth of a Tumour

Sadly, Trish and I were soon to part company on the work front. We often had fairly informal staff meetings with the three radiologists who ran the practice. There were only three employees, two radiographers, one of whom was Trish, and then I was medical secretary and bookkeeper. Unbeknown to me, Trish had planned to say at the next meeting how unfairly paid she thought I was, considering I was also the bookkeeper. She was of course right but it was my place to fight for my rights but she also knew I was no good at this. I was to find myself always being underpaid and undervalued in jobs, part of the legacy of low self-esteem and lack of self-worth from childhood. It would have been a good idea to have been given the heads up beforehand because I would not under any circumstances have condoned this approach. But it just spontaneously came out at the end as 'any other business'. And she said it just like that, and there sat the biggest elephant in the room I have ever seen followed by complete silence and then utter shock from me most of all. The full implication of this was to hit me later. I was sure they would sack her and I knew if they did this, then I too would have to resign as it would be seen that we had collaborated to force a wage rise for me. The other radiographer was left astonished at the outcome. The next day Trish was shown the door and an agency radiographer quickly put in place. I was now left with the dilemma of what to do. I felt the only thing to do was to give notice as the workplace had now become an embarrassment. Having discussed the situation with my husband, he seemed only too delighted as he thought now would be a good time to start a family. I found a temporary job doing bookkeeping

Chapter 4 - Growth of a Tumour

for a small sports club and it wasn't long before I became pregnant, but not before I had started a hypnotherapy course in London. As the pregnancy continued, I continued to study. I worked in my job until the end and then we decided it would be better if I looked after my child myself rather than return to work. I was pleased and relieved at this idea as I wanted to do this job myself rather than share it with a childminder. We had also moved out of London to a dilapidated cottage that we rented for a song but there was a lot to be done to it. My father and I did an astounding renovation job and by the time my son was born we had a lovely small home right in the heart of the country, which is exactly how I had wanted to raise my children.

When my son was born, I had finished the first part of my hypnotherapy diploma and he was born without the use of conventional pain relief as I had used self-hypnosis. This amazed the hospital staff especially in a town in the south of England - London perhaps may have understood it but this was long before the time of the rise in popularity of Hypnobirthing. This was 1991. Monitoring my child's heartbeat, they were flabbergasted to find that just before being born, he was 'sleeping'. I tried to explain that he was in hypnosis but this was considered to be even more strange. Quietly behind the scenes I could hear them getting ready to take him to the special baby unit. It was a difficult birth and, the first time, the ventouse extraction failed as the obstetrician seemed rather incompetent. Eventually, with a struggle, my child was born and, as I already knew, he did not need any special care and my beautiful baby was handed into my arms. My husband was also present for the birth, which culturally for him was most unusual. With my child now in my life, I understood what Brenda had once said to me:

"*It is not marriage that changes your life – it's children.*"

Right from the start he was a demanding baby, he displayed signs of colic in his early weeks. Even when this settled, he would scream for long periods and the health visitor, with many years of experience, had no answers. I bought a baby pouch for him and here he would curl up, snuggle down and go to sleep when I was out walking, shopping and cleaning the house. He seemed to want constant reassurance and, as he grew older, I bought a frame that could be put on my back like a rucksack and he could look out over the top and observe everything I was doing. He never seemed to stop. He slept for only 2 hours at a time and then would scream and demand to get up. His brain could not absorb enough. Once he had snippets of speech, he would perch on my shoulder as I carried him around and point at everything in the room with his favourite words, "and that?" I would reply with the name of each item; he had an unquenchable thirst for a vocabulary he could then express himself with and learn more. He seemed to instinctively know that these names we give to things were the key to opening the wider world. He did not crawl but very soon was on his feet and with a small trolley loaded with toy bricks he raced through the cottage at increasingly dangerous speeds, nearly demolishing the doors as he went. By night he wanted the vacuum cleaner taken apart so he could understand its workings. I do not know how I would have managed a job as well!

Three years later, my second son was born and, fortunately for me at that time, he was calm and self-contained as my older son's behaviour became more and more exhausting even when he started play school. Our doctor suggested trying a course of Ritalin. Fortunately, just at that time I was attending a music class with him in the hope that engaging him in some exuberant entertainment might eventually induce some calm. There I met a mum who passed on some invaluable information about an Osteopathy Centre for Children in Cavendish Square in London that performed cranial osteopathy and she had found it very useful for her colicky baby. I called them up and the following week we were up to London, across on the underground with one child in a front pouch, a pushchair over my shoulder and my older son on a full set of chest reins. They were truly amazing at the Centre. They tested him for allergies and discovered he was allergic to salicylates in fruit, which explained why he had a craving for fresh fruit juices. Stewart, who was in charge of the Centre, assessed him and treated him under the table on the first occasion and Suzie, his second in command, was to see him through his childhood and teenage years and even into adult life. They explained that the ventouse extraction had also caused a great deal of pressure and could even identify the spinal rotation that had followed. This was my first encounter with 'complementary therapy' other than reiki and hypnotherapy and I found it impressive. After sessions, he would come back and sleep soundly and gradually as he attended school his behaviour calmed and his intelligence became apparent. When I found out more about the side effects of Ritalin, I was very glad that I had not gone that route.

Six months after giving birth to my second son, my mother died. Although we only lived three doors away, her visits became less and less and she talked very little about what was happening for her. By this time, she had had bilateral mastectomies and a partial thyroidectomy for Hashimoto's disease. Over the last 50 years, studies have shown that

Chapter 4 - Growth of a Tumour

there is a strong link between breast cancer and thyroid disease but the link, if it was known, was not something that my mother's generation of women were told about. My mother continued to manage her physical and emotional pain with whiskey and was a functioning alcoholic, so getting close to her emotionally never really happened. We did all gather around her bed two days before she died because my older son, although only three, insisted he was going up the road to see Granny. She passed away quickly and fairly peacefully with my father caring for her to the end. I think she was happy to let go of the world that had not afforded her a great deal of enjoyment. Once her children had left home, she seemed to have very little to motivate her. I didn't feel a great deal of sadness at her passing, mainly relief for her, as she had mentally died following her first mastectomy.

Gradually, life settled down and I began to embrace the difference between my two sons, each challenging in their own very different ways. One showed a gift for maths and money and made himself a task to write up to a million, which he did on sheets of A4 paper stuck together with sticky tape and laid out all over the hard surface of the kitchen floor. He was so determined and each day kept on adding more and more numbers. My other son wanted a word tin with lots of books and, like me, found stories magical. He very soon began to write his own. Our lives were filled with *Old Bear* stories, fairy tales from around the world, Aesop's Fables, playing in the woods and making dens. I too finally had a childhood. However, when you have grown up in abuse it is not unusual to attract the same pattern to yourself in adult life because you become conditioned to accept that this is 'normal'. There is familiarity to it and it becomes strangely 'comfortable' because it is all you have known. I was no exception. Although I had travelled more than 5,000 miles to a different country, culture, race and religion, I had remained the same person. Unlike now, I was unaware then of the tendency to repeat the attraction of abusive behavioural patterns to oneself and the road ahead was to be hard, lonely and very rocky. There had been some obvious signs of changes within our marriage once we came to live in England. But it was easier for me to normalise them and see them as cultural differences. The date 18th March proved to be as inauspicious for my marriage as it had been for my birth. The old patterns of rejection and abuse that had haunted me in my childhood had now reappeared. I started to see that whereas some aspects of his behaviour could have been attributed to culture, the narcissistic ones could not. As my

children grew, these became more apparent. One of my mother's favourite phrases very aptly described my situation:
"You have made your bed, now lie in it."

I learnt how to overcome exhaustion, how to find money from thin air, how to give until you have nothing more to give, how to make these little people feel that they were the most special things on the earth plane and so much more. Acquiring these skills also came without a manual of how to do it. I only had my own upbringing as a guide, which was as good as having nothing at all. I was determined I was going to do things differently.

As my second son grew, he showed a tendency to asthma and when he was prescribed a Ventolin inhaler, I went straight to the Osteopathy Centre where he was treated by an extremely gifted therapist from Sri Lanka and gradually the allergic reactions subsided. Money was in short supply with no income now coming in from me, so when my older son went to playschool, I looked for work. I was offered a cleaning job and before long I was covering the cleaning and ironing for many of the families in the village where both adults worked. It meant I could take my younger son with me, leave him to play on the floors as I moved him around the rooms as I cleaned. By night I did the ironing as they slept. As time went by, Rosemary, who ran the children's playschool, did everything she could to assist me. She offered an extra free weekly afternoon session, and gave me a cleaning and gardening job at the nursery. We later became close friends and throughout my tumultuous years, she was always there with either an ear to listen, a warm meal, a glass of wine or even a peaceful place to sleep. How precious it is to have this kind of friend. Words cannot express my gratitude.

By now, my older son had had a psychological assessment which put him into the top 2% of the population with regards to his intelligence. It was suggested that private schooling would be the best way forward. This was completely out of our league. However, it didn't stop me looking at the fees and getting brochures for the private schools in our area. Not long after the assessment was carried out, out of the blue I was contacted by Sun Life of Canada with whom I had started saving a private pension some years previously. They had caught up with the fact that I had not been working and my husband had been paying my pension without my realising that this could only be done by me. This meant that a handsome sum was due for payback. My immediate thought was, this is happening just in time to enrol my son and pay his

Chapter 4 - Growth of a Tumour

first term's fees at a private school. I find it uncanny sometimes how the universe seems to provide just as you feel that there is no way forward.

There are things about an incompatible marriage that are best left unsaid. From my point of view, I see no reason in compounding the pain and misery of those years by writing bitter words and lengthy descriptions of narcissistic and abusive behaviour. I do not wish to leave this as a remembrance for my two beautiful children. I tried to always make them my priority throughout this difficult, lonely, and painful time and that meant making extremely hard personal sacrifices, particularly when financial reasons and the children's long-term futures were the main deciding factors for me to stay in such a situation. In hindsight, I do not think I could have done anything differently and, rather than regret, I now prefer to accept it and see it as part of my life's journey.

Sadly, their young lives involved the experience of a refuge. They were five and eight and I was struggling to keep us safe. On its positive side, this experience also came with the generosity of my brother who paid for us to fly to Canada for safety. My sister, whom I had no love for as a child, now opened her doors to us and gave us a temporary home. She did not know at that time what it meant to lay your head on a pillow and sleep for many hours without fear. I remain deeply grateful. Before the trip I made legal history by being allowed to take my children out of regular schooling to go abroad for 6 weeks. My brother-in-law was a teacher in Canada so in the court I could prove that they could be home schooled. Once on Canadian soil, my young son in particular blossomed and went to a local kindergarten and both boys learnt to swim at the local YMCA where my sister fixed up free membership for them. As I recovered during this time, one key thing which stands out for me was when I went to the local hairdresser and had my long waist-length hair cut really short. As I watched my hair fall to the floor, it was like a rite of passage and a shedding of my femininity. I made a vow to myself, as I had as a child, that no one would ever take my mind even if they had broken my body over and over again. I now felt comfortably depersonalised and asexual and with this new persona I felt safe. I later learnt that coping mechanisms like this are common in women who have undergone abuse.

On my forced return from Canada because of the court order, the children returned to their school and I looked for more work. With my nursing background and previous medical secretarial training, I landed a job at a local GP surgery. I started as an audio typist even though three weeks after starting, the regular secretary went on holiday and I was quickly 'promoted' into her position to cover her but without the salary. Here was the same old boring lesson presenting itself again. When the secretary got back, she realised that I had been to a training centre before taking the job and was trained in Word, which was the next step up from Word Perfect. This would be the system they would have to change over to in the near future to upgrade their computer system. She addressed this issue with the doctors, saying she feared I would leave if I didn't get the title and salary of a secretary. Eventually, I was given this and it helped to cover the next lot of school fees. As time went by and practice managers came and went, a new role emerged, namely that of Medical Notes Summariser. This involved taking old paper medical records, reading them and putting them onto the computer with a READ code. This enabled all the records to now be on an electronic system. It also allowed audits to be run so that you would know how many patients in your practice had, for example, diabetes or heart conditions or different types of cancers. This could be paired up with how many patients were on certain medications. Because of my nursing background and typing skills, I was offered the job and I thoroughly enjoyed it. It was mentally stimulating and absorbing. After about my first thousand notes, I noticed something extremely important that now more than twenty years later is finally being acknowledged as being 'significant'. I realised I could almost predict the outcome of a person's disease by looking at the psychological causes that led up to it. In those days, very thorough notes were written by GPs and consultants. In particular, the GPs were almost considered a family friend so any underlying family issues were discussed more openly than today when you have seven minutes if you are lucky and you can only discuss one issue at a time. Usually the most important one is when the patient has their hand on the door handle to leave and they say:

"Oh, by the way doctor..."

But that one gets left until next time and by next time they may have decided not to discuss it because of embarrassment or deciding it isn't relevant after all.

I was able to see that psychological trauma and depression over a long period of time usually resulted in a very relevant disease or illness. For example, women who had gone through divorce or abusive relationships or trauma around their children growing up, tended to manifest breast cancer or gynaecological diseases. Irritable bowel disease is also a disease of our lifetime frequently caused by holding stress in the gut area, a poor

Chapter 4 - Growth of a Tumour

diet and shallow breathing. Often after years of investigations where nothing was found initially, gradually in later years, the disease finally presented itself. It was as if the psychological wounding caused the physical manifestation of the disease. Similarly, men who retired early from work or lost their partner seemed to develop prostate cancer as if their role as a man was over. I would free-type certain relevant pieces of information including clarifying if someone had had a depressive episode by adding what had led up to it. It wasn't long before the GP overseeing my work asked me why I was putting in so much 'psychological' information as if this was not relevant. Clearly, the link between mind and body had a long way to go when it came to the medical world. I remember replying that one day they may see the importance and now they finally are. As the NHS mental health services reach crisis point and cancers and diabetes are reaching epidemic proportions, it may be relevant to look at the statistics: 1 in 4 children suffer abuse in their life; 1 in 4 (though realistically 1 in 3 would be a closer figure) women suffer domestic abuse and 1 in 6 men; 1 in 4 women are taking antidepressants and the suicide rate in young men is ever rising. All it requires is to put the correct READ codes onto the patient's records and the results will become evident particularly if it then goes on to look at cancers such as breast and ovarian cancers in women. The most relevant thing I have found is that, for many people nowadays, life tends to limp from one crisis to another. There is not enough sweetness in their lives with little time for relaxation and friends other than on Facebook, so it comes in the form of buns, fizzy drinks, too much wine and chocolate. Eventually this causes the body to go into overload on sugar and forms a rich soupy acid environment ideal for disease.

As my children grew, so did the need for a bigger salary so I applied for another part-time job that fitted in with my job at the medical centre. By this time, I had acquired an Advanced Diploma in Counselling and a degree from the Open University in Psychology and I took a job as a support worker in a women's refuge. Here my personal knowledge of domestic abuse was invaluable as were my counselling skills, and parts of the life puzzle were beginning to slot into place. The job involved an hour of travel each way and leaving early in the morning. It was hard juggling both jobs, returning in the evening to pick up the boys from school, going home to cook supper and getting everything prepared for the next day – but like a hamster on a treadmill I kept going. I was young and energetic and never got ill apart from a yearly cold as winter approached. Just like the discoveries I was making from my note summaries, I too was a ticking time bomb but I didn't make the connection.

As the boys reached the ages of 11 and 14, it was decided that they were now old enough to be taken on a trip to India to see their grandparents. A proposed visit to India several years earlier had been the very reason why the children and I had finished up in a refuge. My husband could not have afforded for the children to stay in good accommodation in India when they were younger. Since it had been deemed my responsibility alone to prevent them from becoming sick while there, I had refused to be a party to this and my decision for us not to go came with its repercussions. I had good reason for this decision because in spite of my strong constitution, I had experienced several months of ill health while living there. Reluctantly, now the children were older, I had to agree to this visit but not without trepidation.

For our trip, each person chose a place they would like to visit and the choices were as diverse as the family members. My husband chose to visit one of the oldest Hindu temples in India. My older son's choice was Mumbai to see Marine Drive where all the stars and the wealthy lived. My younger son wanted to see the tigers in the Corbett National Park and I chose Dharamshala - the current home of the Dalai Lama. It was a marathon amount of travelling, particularly the journey high into the mountains to reach Dharamshala. We hired a taxi and to say that the journey was hair-raising was putting it mildly as blind bend after blind bend was negotiated at speed, up and up into the mountains. Anyone who knows Indian mountain roads will understand that there is no barrier to stop you careering down the mountain if you get it wrong. It is not unusual to see the remains of an old car or bus turned on its side far down the mountain side as you look out of the window of your vehicle. I think at this stage the rest of the family thought I had lost the plot taking them into such inhospitable territory and on such a dangerous journey. I have to confess, I had no idea of the altitude we would be climbing to and, at the time the holiday was planned, it was assumed that it was a relatively easy road journey. Unfortunately, as the hours passed, both boys started to get sick from their earlier stay at the Corbett National Park. Although the food was prepared freshly, I am sure in spite of saying that the salad needed to be washed in cooled, boiled water, this didn't happen. We reached Dharamshala in the evening and went to Chonor House in McLeod Ganj, a beautiful guest house made famous by the actor Richard Gere, who had stayed there

Chapter 4 - Growth of a Tumour

during his visit. Fortunately, we had booked in advance because as night fell, both children became violently ill. Whenever I arrive in India I always go straight to the pharmacy and pick up metronidazole (Flagyl) tablets which are the only thing that will clear 'Delhi Belly' in an emergency situation. I had also packed in my suitcase a set of cooking rings, a saucepan, some instant soup sachets, packets of bread sticks and malt biscuits. Its rather like a wacky version of the game 'I'm going to London and in my suitcase I am taking ...' only this one is I am going to Delhi and in my suitcase I am taking everything I can possibly think of with me so that I do not spend my entire holiday in the toilet. I would highly recommend this version of the game to anyone planning a visit to India!

Once in the hotel room, I set to work and even remembered what I had learnt in my science lessons, that because I was at high altitude the water needed to boil for longer. As soon as the boys kept the tablets down, after 48 hours they slowly began to recover. Regular feeding with soups made with clean water, breadsticks and dried biscuits helped to settle them down and give them some strength in their bodies, which so quickly become depleted with a diarrheal disease. Ultimately, my fear about taking them to India when they were younger was not unfounded. As I sat up the first night with my patients, nursing was not without its rewards as it gave me the opportunity to get to closely observe what I would call the most beautiful room in the world I have ever stayed in. Every room in the guest house is unique and decorated from floor to ceiling with murals according to a particular Tibetan theme. The colours are sublime and absolutely exquisite, transporting you into a world of fantasy and ancient story-telling. I would love one day to go back and stay in the guest house again and revisit the whole area, this time truly imbibing it all to myself.

We had four days planned in the mountains so as the boys recovered, we went for a walk in the mountain air. We noticed that a crowd was gathered outside the Dalai Lama Temple and discovered that he was in residence and shortly about to give a discourse. In those days, you did not need to make a booking to sit and listen so we sat down and within a few minutes of taking our seats on the floor he came into the temple. For me, this personal experience of sitting high in the mountains in a Buddhist temple was the fulfilment of my teenage dream. The energy was more than invigorating, it was intoxicating. All around me, my senses were heightened by the rich colours of gold, red, orange and jade. I am sure if you have to be in exile, then Dharamshala is the closest you will get to feeling like you are in Tibet and ultimately 'the roof of the world'. Its altitude is approximately 1457 metres and surrounded by snow-capped mountains. Its beauty is also reflected in the people, tanned from the mountain air and sun, greeting each other with a bow and a calm respect, honouring the light within each other. I had come all this way to visit this wonderland and the Dalai Lama just happened to be here at the same time! As he entered the temple with his entourage, there was an immediate stillness that descended on the crowd and his presence filled the temple. As he sat down, a smile broke out on his face and his sense of fun and playfulness lit up his features. He jokingly said in Tibetan and then English that everyone was sitting so solemnly as if a great wisdom was going to be imparted and he was wondering who they were expecting. In his playfulness, one got the impression he was trying to say:

"Why are you taking this all so seriously?"

The discourse was to last for several hours and there was a means provided to hear the translation. I would have liked nothing better than to spend my afternoon there but the rest of the family had different ideas. The two boys soon became restless and asked to go and my husband looked at me as if to say why was I still sitting there as there was nothing more to be gained from staying? This was neither the time nor place to have a discussion and say that I wished to stay and listen and I felt embarrassed and frustrated that I had to get up and walk out of the temple when the discourse had only just begun. From this episode, I learnt that it is important to visit such places either alone or with like-minded people so that the experience can be felt to the full without having to think of other people's needs when they are simply not vibrating on the same wavelength. Nevertheless, the seed had been planted and, in the future, it would once again trigger an important connection with my choice of recovery and how remembering past events would be the key to unlock the future. I have realised over the years that nothing ever happens by chance.

Scientists have found that it takes many years to grow a tumour and I would say in my case it took approximately seven trauma-filled years to make two tumours. Bringing the children up had been no easy task and when I was told in 2016 by a 'seer' that I had had cancer three times, I think this statement was not wrong. I had just overcome it each time but now events were escalating out of my control as no doubt were the cancer cells. As if the previous years had not been bad enough, even more trauma was to come and this became relentless from 2007 onwards. We

Chapter 4 - Growth of a Tumour

left our country cottage just prior to going to the refuge, because of the lack of a heating system, and then lived in horrible conditions in local authority housing, for more than seven years. We finally moved house in May 2007. I packed up single handed with occasional help from my older son, who was sitting his GCSEs at the time. I organised a friend to move us as it was within the same village. Although it was stressful, it was a relief to move from the environment we were in to a place where the boys could finally each have a room of their own. However, shortly after that came the financial crisis. As money grew tighter and my husband's resentment grew regarding the buying of the house at the wrong time, he chose to remove the school fees from both boys. It was a time at the school when many families were crumbling under financial losses and the school could not save them all. I knew it would take a miracle to salvage this one. By the time my husband had written a letter to the school withdrawing both boys, there was nowhere my older son could have applied as the good college places were already taken and no more applicants would be taken in. It was designated my responsibility to sort the boys out. Well, miracles can and do happen. I made an appointment at the boy's school before it closed for the summer holidays. I explained many issues from the past and the headmaster, after a lot of negotiation with the authorities, gave my older boy a full scholarship, something which had never happened in the school's history. This left me to manage the fees for my second son in instalments. I was entering one of the hardest phases of my life but society has taught women today that they must be 'Superwoman' and this was one job I was up for. I didn't earn enough to pay back the fees but there had to be a way and I was determined to find it.

My main coping mechanism at this time was my weekly trip to the Spiritualist Church. In my workplace, I had struck up a friendship with a colleague and it is not unusual for like-minded people to quickly recognise each other. I had been missing meditation from my days of being with Trish and going to Ruth's workshops, and also I was having a deep desire to reconnect with the spiritual world. Every Friday after work, I went. I differed from many of the 'experienced' mediums in the group in that I did not often get a direct link with the spirit world as I had done when I was a child. My meditations, however, were beautiful and profound. They would take me into the world of shamanism and flying on the back of an eagle over lands and seas. The colours of these other worlds were like none seen on the earth plane. They were bright and pure and of a different vibration. I particularly felt an affinity for purple and would sit and meditate sometimes with this pure colour pouring through as if from the area of the third eye. I was visited by guides, in particular a Tibetan guide dressed in orange robes. I could never see his face, only a large black obsidian mirror that he would sit in front of. I requested one day to know why I could never see his face and I was informed that he had been beheaded when Tibet had been invaded. His mirror had been split in half and used to kill him because he had refused to divulge the spiritual information that the monks held. In one session at the church, the leader introduced trance mediumship and invited me to take part. I found this was something that came naturally to me and I received some very profound messages. Towards the end of my time at the church my guide delivered to me very clearly one night that if the people in the church and all those on the earth plane did not raise their vibrational levels considerably higher they would not be able to survive the changes that were now taking place. Our two group leaders eventually left because of ill health and, although I was asked if I wanted to take over, I declined as I felt that this was not where my talents lay. Over the years since leaving the church I came to hear that several other members of our group had become ill and, sadly, my work colleague who had introduced me to the church died suddenly in a car accident. I felt guilty and burdened by what I was hearing, particularly as I had delivered such a message, but my guide informed me that, like the falcon, I had been designated the messenger, nothing else.

Once I left the group, I no longer meditated as the home environment was not conducive to this and there was no other group that I felt I wanted to be affiliated with. Also, life events were again accelerating.

I was barely on my feet following the school fees episode, when the next event took over. The atmosphere at the refuge where I worked had always been toxic but it now become increasingly more abusive to work in. The two bullies in the organisation were in the top posts. One was the CEO and the other my immediate boss. My boss was eventually removed from the organisation, by the CEO, for bullying. She was indeed a bully but she was also the ideal scapegoat to mask what was happening further up the ladder. To my way of thinking, both of them should have been removed at the same time as neither were fit for purpose working with vulnerable women who were in refuge having fled from perpetrators of domestic abuse. These two people in charge behaved no differently towards their staff, using similar abusive tactics.

Chapter 4 - Growth of a Tumour

They would play one member of staff off against another, wrongly accuse staff of not doing their jobs properly, bawl colleagues out in front of each other, send abusive emails and make sure staff were never able to take time off in lieu or paid overtime for the many extra hours they worked. Not surprisingly the turnover of staff reflected what was going on in the organisation. It is astonishing what goes on in workplaces and nobody dares to challenge it. I assisted my older colleague, then in her sixties, as she was brought before a tribunal for trumped-up charges purely because she had too many years' experience and had a 'clear' vision of what was going on. She nearly had a heart attack as a result of this and I knew she had no chance of winning against such odds. Shortly after this episode, her husband died and she left the job. I knew it was time for me also to get out as I would be the next to be targeted and I did not want my future to be tarnished through no fault of my own. My crime would have been that I supported someone who had been made a victim because of serious issues that were being camouflaged. The CEO was eventually removed but that was not for some time to come. The biggest blow to me was that I had just received a salary increase which had raised my income to a level which would have helped considerably towards the school fees. Now, no matter what, I would be losing this income. I was damned if I stayed and damned if I went. I knew I had to leave fast. It was like watching the same patterns in reverse that had happened with Trish all those years previously, when she had advocated for me at work, and it was also a precursor and a warning to what would ensue for me in the future.

Just as I thought things couldn't get much worse, they did. My younger son did something that was to have far-reaching effects on all our lives. Years ago, it would have been seen as a silly schoolboy prank. That was all it was but we are living in a society that has no forgiveness and one stupid mistake can follow you for the rest of your life. It also resulted in the two brothers not talking to each other for years. In the early stages, they would not even sit at the same table with each other and the food had to be carried upstairs to one of them at mealtimes. The stress levels in the house were now unbearable. The only saving grace in my life was my beautiful Red Setter, Iona, who we had bought for my older son's eighteenth birthday. I finally had my real dog that I could curl up with in bed, cry into her coat and receive the most amazing love and warmth I have ever known. I could not have seen my way through those years without her.

I rapidly handed my notice in once my colleague had finished her tribunal and within weeks of leaving found a replacement job with an agency. It was exactly the same type of work in a refuge with more outreach work and closer to home. My boss was lovely and in time I managed to fit in with the permanent staff. They had developed their own way of doing things and found change rather challenging. However, it wasn't long before the refuge was taken over again by this new breed of 'corporate woman' that seems to be rife in organisations managing women's social needs and charities. I call them 'corporate women' because they appear to be under the illusion that they have been given the task of running a large, profitable company which in reality is very different from running a women's refuge. They would most probably fail in the corporate world as they carry only an insincere air of power about them in order to mask their own insecurities. This results in using their frustrations with their own weaknesses and failures for destructive control over others. I have now observed this happen three times, resulting in all the best staff leaving the organisations and peanuts being paid to new staff to fill these roles of support workers. So 'corporate woman' swept in having 'won the tender' by offering the cheapest deal. It mattered not whether the deal presented to the authorities was tenable; it was cheaper than the one before. We would as usual have to apply for our own jobs and since these were on offer in the form of a new job title and a contract with a lower salary for more hours, we all left as was the desired goal.

Shortly after leaving in 2010, I landed a part-time job working with high-risk cases of domestic abuse. This was an extremely stressful job and probably carries the same stress levels as working for the police. Life was full of change on the home front also. My oldest son was now at university and my younger son was finally going to college, which didn't require fees but I was still paying off the school fees which had now become like a mortgage.

As the next few years passed, my older son moved to London for work and my young son with a great deal of stress managed some incredible A level results and obtained a place at university. But this was not before life dealt its final blows. In 2012 tensions were mounting at the GP surgery where I had given 14 years of dedicated work. A new manager took over and it was clear he had some deep unresolved personal issues. He announced very soon after taking up the post that he could see the day when all the part-time workers would be gone and the jobs would be taken over by two full-time workers. He won over

Chapter 4 - Growth of a Tumour

hearts and minds by bringing in doughnuts for coffee time and offering lifts in bad weather, but it was not long before the free coffee we had always enjoyed suddenly needed to be paid for and the biscuits were brought out only for the doctors. A new division of 'them' and 'us' began and with it a feeling of deep unrest. It reminded me of Orwell's book *Animal Farm*. One by one, the old members of staff whose faces didn't fit had charges trumped up against them if they didn't decide to leave because they 'wanted to retire'. My real difficulty in life is that I have this uncanny way of intuitively knowing what is going to happen long before it happens but my mistake is that I don't get out in time. When my turn came, I handed in my notice after informing them in writing that I knew exactly what was going on. I even kept a log and sometimes pictures of all the trumped-up charges that were being constructed and I recorded the meetings. I knew I could not win because top lawyers were brought in from London for the Tribunal to hear the case I had brought against the manager and this ultimately involved the GPs since they had appointed him. However, I was determined that if nothing else it would put an end finally to what was being done and that no more staff would suffer the same fate. In 2013 I lost the battle for my own job but won the war, as I later learnt that no more staff had been forced out of their jobs in such an unjust way, even though several more at that time had been selected for 'culling'. Making health centres into a profitable business seems somewhat bizarre to me. Even the medication costs have to be finally picked up by someone. There is rarely a sense of the patient getting better in the long term on these products, so profitability is not going to happen even if you ply the patient with more drugs to counteract the side effects of the original ones given. The patient will eventually require more and more care and become less productive as we are seeing in today's elderly population. There is no doubt that in my early years in the NHS, there was a lot of unnecessary wastage and accountability is crucial in all organisations. Nevertheless, it is important when applying the business model to a social establishment that the original ethos behind the organisation's intention is not eroded.

With my 14 years of loyalty behind me and little to show for it, there was more to come. My father's health was deteriorating, my husband had moved abroad to work and my older son had a motorcycle accident. It was a wet, cold night and he had phoned me while he was at a petrol station on the motorway to say that he would be home in 20 minutes. When he gave me a time, he was always accurate. Between the time of the phone call and those 20 minutes he was to encounter an accident up ahead of him that meant a pile-up was beginning to happen. In those wet road conditions and travelling at speed he was unable to slow down enough and his bike began to skid. He decided that to part company with his bike was the only way he could save his life and he wasn't wrong. He bounced down the motorway in his leathers at 70 mph, slowly decelerating. The times he had spent looking at YouTube videos of motorcycle accidents had paid off and he walked away with bruised knees thanks also to a lorry driver coming up behind him. He saw what was happening and swerved the truck protectively across the lane to prevent any traffic hitting my son. Even his laptop in his rucksack still on his back had survived and the paramedics going to the accident up ahead picked him up on the way! I was alone when I took the phone call from him from the hospital. I had been watching the clock minutes tick by and I couldn't bring myself to think or feel what might be happening as it got later and later for his return. The culmination of all the years of stress finally came to a head and this was, in the words of the song, my 'total eclipse of the heart'. I didn't allow myself to feel. I didn't want to feel anymore. The pain of life was now getting too great and I was shutting down. I got into the car and like a robot I drove and picked him up from the hospital. This place of 'non-feeling' had now become so much part of my life I didn't even shed a tear. I put my arms around him but I JUST COULDN'T FEEL ANYTHING.

It wasn't long after the accident that my son's job moved him permanently to the United States and now, for the first time, I was alone in the house – just me and my dog. I was exhausted and the job I was now doing fulltime with high-risk cases of domestic abuse carried a huge amount of stress and responsibility. There were three of us to cover most of Hampshire and on the horizon was looming yet again a tender to provide a cheaper service. My boss felt if we worked hard and delivered a good service then it would eventually pay off. I held a different view from her. Hard work and good service were no longer in vogue. She was living in a bygone era. Fortunately, at this time my good friend Rosemary from the children's nursery days was looking for a trekking companion for Peru and I was greatly in need of a holiday. So, having withdrawn a small pension fund, I decided it was time to have some fun and it might all look rosier on my return. How wrong could I have been.

CHAPTER 5

Diagnosis

I arrived back to England from Peru on 9th May 2014. I had had the time of my life. Before going, I had been doing Zumba classes at the local sports centre in preparation for my hike. In addition, I ran in the mornings with Iona and walked for at least 40 minutes with her in the evenings. On weekends, Rosemary and I had been going up and down some steep hills, breaking in my hiking boots and learning to use my poles in preparation for the Salkantay Pass at an altitude of some 3,000 metres or more. It had been some serious trekking and I had been looking forward to the sheer excitement of it. After 14 days of experiencing a beautiful culture, stunning sights, watching condors fly and relaxing in hot tubs in luxury lodges with exquisite food, it was back to earth with a bump. I was due back to work on the Monday morning. I collected Iona from my colleague who had been looking after her and returned to an empty house. My husband was still living in India, my older son was away working in the US and my younger son was in the Midlands at university.

There was a pile of mail waiting on the floor and I picked it up ready to look through it once I had settled Iona and unpacked. I noticed that there seemed to be an awful lot of NHS letters, but I had done my bowel cancer screen before I left, which had come back all clear. The only other one was the mammogram result. Later that evening I began to open the letters. The first was dated 1st May 2014 from the Director of Breast Screening stating that there were "grounds for concern or uncertainty". I had already been offered an appointment on 7th May but had missed this because of my holiday. A new appointment was booked for 15th May

2014 at 13.00. I tried to push the niggling suspicion that something was wrong to one side. When my sister had been diagnosed with cancer two years previously and she had written an email with everything she was having done and tracing the genetic links, I had had one of my intuitive voices in my head at that time with:

"You will be next."

I chose not to listen. My appointment was for further screening, and biopsy if necessary. I went alone. I am the sort of person who needs to be on their own when facing a crisis so that I only have to deal with my own emotions and not other people's who might be struggling with what to say to me at that time. The appointment was a horror story from start to finish. My screening done, I met with the radiologist who was about as subtle as a kick in the crutch. She pinned up the results and announced that there were two lumps that would need biopsies. When I asked, "Would this need a mastectomy?" she replied that this was something I would need to discuss with the surgeon but mastectomy was highly likely. She applied local anaesthetic to my left breast and barely gave it time to work. There was no explanation of what she was going to do. She assumed that her patients read the leaflets and she didn't know I had been a nurse. There was no eye contact, which was a theme that seemed to follow me right the way through my NHS experience. The second lump was on the left outer quadrant much further away from the larger one and clearly the anaesthetic had not taken effect in this area. As she took the biopsy, I let out a yell. I do not consider myself a wimp, having had two children without any pain relief other than self-hypnosis but this was absolutely excruciating. I was having breast tissue excised without a local anaesthetic. She did not even apologise and I could see the look of both surprise and pity on the nurse's face as she stroked my arm. She was also aware that I had come on my own. Although this experience was miserable, I can look back and I am grateful for it because if the NHS staff had been different I might, in my vulnerability, have been swayed into making a different decision.

I came home that night so sore and bruised. I felt frightened and alone and there was no one to talk to. I left my bra on all night as I could feel the soreness begin to increase. I lay in bed, cuddled with Iona and cried. Sensing my distress, she licked me and cuddled closer. Next day, I went to work as usual. Fortunately, it was Friday and I had the weekend free. At this stage, my colleague suspected there was something wrong as she is quite psychic, and also I was beginning to realise that in spite of a fabulous holiday I did not look well. I still was not ready to disclose what

Chapter 5 - Diagnosis

was happening. When you give something a voice, it makes it real and the moment you say "I have breast cancer" out loud to someone, then you own it and gradually your mind has to start to process these words. The bruising and soreness of my breast became worse and I was horrified to look at it as it went through all its stages of colour changes until, after several weeks, it was finally back to normality. I started to think about what it would look like if I had to see scarring every day of my life and I choked back the scream that was rising in my throat. I wanted to go out into a wood somewhere I would not be heard and scream and scream but in the overpopulated south of England, I doubt I could have found such a place. I knew with the NHS cutbacks and later, from what other women of my age had said, that I would not be a priority for reconstruction surgery. Not only that, I am not sure I could have mentally coped with the skin grafting that would have been required. I am terrified of surgery, having seen too much as a nurse.

I had been given the definitive diagnosis, so I knew there was no need to await the results. With our family history and the intuitive voice I had received, I knew the score. On 22nd May I went to see the consultant surgeon allocated to me. Again I went alone, took a book and pretended to read it. I then noticed another woman enter the waiting area with, presumably, her husband. I recognised her from the recall appointment so no doubt she had received the same news. Hospitals always make me feel sick, they smell of dirt, disease and death and I find it difficult to believe that I once worked in one for more than four years. My name was called quite quickly and I entered the surgeon's consultation room. He was fairly small, dark haired and wore a dark suit. I did not see much of his face because when I entered the room – he was looking at his computer screen with what looked like a PowerPoint presentation. At least that was my memory of that day. He offered me a chair, addressed me by name and began to speak:

"Unfortunately, you have multifocal breast cancer in the left breast that will require a mastectomy. There is no spread to the lymph nodes as far as we can see but some tissue may be taken at surgery for confirmation. Here is the prognosis at this time. As you can see from the screen, there is a good five-year survival rate for your type of cancer. At least 90% survive for 5 years and many more go on until 10 years."

My consultant did not look at me throughout this PowerPoint presentation. I could have been Paddington Bear sitting in the chair. Gradually he drew to a close on his business presentation regarding the likely outcome of my left mammary gland which had nurtured both of my children, and I knew I needed to leave the room quickly as a wave of nausea washed over me. How could you ever explain to someone who only saw a body that it was not the cancer at all but the thought of looking in the mirror at a large scar and a lopsided body. Even worse, I would have to confront daily the physical manifestation of self-destructive behaviour. I would no longer be able to wear my invisibility cloak because everything that had happened to me throughout my life, would now be all too visible. Every morning when I took a shower, the abuse would be visible to me. I knew I had brought these tumours about by negative automatic thinking. This type of thinking begins as a result of being conditioned with words in childhood, such as 'you will never amount to anything; you are no good; ugly; fat; stupid; useless' – to name but a few. These words frequently become an inner monologue and, over the years, the 'you' changes to 'I'. The nature of this internal conversation eventually becomes too painful to listen to, so the next level of self-harming begins such as excessive alcohol consumption or comfort eating in order to soothe the pain and reduce the ever-increasing possibility of suicide. The truth was now there for me to face. I had 'thought' those tumours and had closed and sealed my pain into a solid encapsulated form which were, in fact, my own cells. Hard lumps of solid pain put there by my own emotional thoughts which had finally become a daily mantra of:

"*I can't stand this anymore.*"

"*I really don't want to do this anymore.*"

"*If this is all that there is, I don't want to be here anymore.*"

Well, now I finally knew nearly fifty years on where thoughts go to; wherever you want them to go to is the answer! To manifest whatever you want them to manifest – cancer if that is your focus.

I felt sure that the man before me was not going to be interested in any of this. For many of the medical professionals, the body is a body, which clearly now had mechanically gone wrong, more than likely due to the genetic predisposition of my mother's side of the family to manifest breast cancer. I was aware that he had come to the close of his presentation and I suddenly found myself saying:

"*What happens if you don't want any of this?*"

Slowly this penetrated through to him and finally he swivelled his chair and looked at me. I mean actually looked and saw me. I detected for a fleeting moment a look of pity in his eyes. He had made the human connection but did not dare to sustain it for long. How could you? Given the job you were doing. Being the surgeon was the easy bit. Making the

Chapter 5 – Diagnosis

human connection to announce what most people perceive as a death sentence is not. He addressed me by name and then said:

"*We don't have all the answers you know.*"

I remember thinking then:

"*Actually, you don't have any as this is exactly what my mother went through. The only difference this time is that there are somewhat regulated doses following the experimental treatment that people have gone through in the past.*"

He again reiterated the survival rates of what he had shown me and basically insinuated that with statistics like that, why would I want to refuse such a pleasing outcome? I briefly explained why this was not an option I would take. His reply was that with two lumps particularly the larger one, it would not be long before I would get symptoms of pain and that spread was highly likely if I did not take the necessary action. He talked about the "little old ladies' option" which was anastrozole or tamoxifen for those people who were too frail for surgery and this might slow the tumour down by removing the oestrogen from the body as my tumours were oestrogen dependent. Otherwise this treatment was generally an ongoing one following the usual conventional treatment, to help prevent the cancer recurring. I was asked if I would like some more time to consider this option and we settled on 3 weeks and to return to see him then with my final decision. There was of course the option to change my mind at any time if I wished to reconsider the surgical route. As in all of my care in the NHS, it was the nurses who were warm, caring and comforting and I was taken aside after the consultation, given a file and some leaflets and one was even kind enough to suggest I could have a free car park pass for my follow-up appointments.

With my head in a turmoil and a scream and a feeling of wanting to vomit rising in my throat I left the hospital. I was in a daze and I had no one to run things by. I had chosen not to tell any of my family or anyone else as I knew deep down no one could support me. It was a decision only I could make and I didn't want anyone else telling me about all the people they knew who had had this done and were fine now. I knew I wouldn't be if I did have it done. I knew I would regret it, and I just could not look at this mutilation day after day. The biopsy alone and the bruising and swelling was enough. I had felt so disgusted just looking at it in the mirror. I came home that evening and had already got a prior engagement with Rosemary. We had arranged to see a performance of *A Curious Incident of the Dog in the Night-Time* as a live broadcast from the National Theatre. It was in our usual local village hall and although I knew that this was not the night to tell her, I fully meant to at some stage. Maybe at the end of the evening, I thought. However, the opportunity was not to arise as she informed me that her faithful dog of 12 years had been put to sleep as she had been diagnosed with a brain tumour – what an ending we had both had to a perfect holiday. I sat watching the performance, which was magnificent, particularly the lights used on the glass floor, but every so often this voice would begin in my head:

"You have breast cancer you know and if you don't treat it you will die."

I kept squashing the voice down and returning to the performance in front of me. It was a memorable performance for more reasons than one.

On the afternoon of 17th June, I had a further appointment with my breast surgeon. It was decision day as to whether I still wanted to refuse surgery and commence on anastrozole. Prior to this I had found out that it was advisable to have a DEXA scan to check bone density as clearly this medication was likely to have an effect on the bones long term. I had to investigate all this for myself and request it from the consultant, who informed me that my GP would be responsible for arranging it. It was a brief meeting with the breast surgeon and I informed him again that I did not wish to have surgery, radiotherapy or chemotherapy but I would try the 'hormone therapy'. He told me he would inform my GP and the medication could be picked up from my local surgery. He wished me all the best and that was the last I was to see of him. As I left the hospital, I felt such an overpowering relief, almost elation, knowing that I didn't have to return to this environment again. It smelt so gross and I couldn't escape fast enough.

This time I chose to go by train and bus to the appointment as driving is not my forte at the best of times and I thought it better not to have to think about rush-hour traffic. Since I had walked Iona before leaving home, I didn't need to rush. My husband was also back from India to attend a tribunal and would then go back after a few weeks to continue with his business ventures. I was glad he would have a distraction that night and be busy talking about the events of his day particularly, if like most tribunals, it was unlikely to go in the employee's favour.

As I travelled back on the bus, I began to think about what the end of all this would be like. Would I struggle to leave life and therefore endure great pain or would I let go as my mother had done? It wasn't death but the way it would happen that concerned me the most. Fortunately, my children were not around me at this time so I did not need to tell anyone and that was the way I wanted it until I had made a

Chapter 5 - Diagnosis

clear decision for me about what I would do. As I got off the bus and went to go to the train station, there began a very clear auditory intuitive voice more powerful than I had ever experienced before, that was to be my guide throughout this journey:

"*You need to go to Waterstones book shop. Go to the first floor and there you will find a book to help you.*"

I did exactly as was suggested and went to the Health section. There, among the glossy paperbacks by well-known authors, I found an unattractive, dark maroon, hardback book entitled *Radical Remission* by Dr Kelly Turner. It looked as though it would be more at home in a university library as a specialist book. The author at that time had started the Radical Remission Project in the United States and the book was the result of a year-long trip around the world, researching alternative healers and cancer survivors. There was certainly nothing about the book at that time that would suggest one day the author would become a *New York Times* bestselling author, screenwriter and producer as a result of this research. I had never heard of her and the book had only just been published, interestingly, on 18th March 2014. It seemed strange that such a book was on a shelf in Waterstones in a relatively small town. I lifted the book down from the shelf and knew instinctively this was the one that I was meant to read. I began reading it on the train home that evening and spent most of the night awake devouring its contents. It gave descriptions of remissions that occurred when Western conventional medicine was either not used at all or when it has failed the patient completely and they were now in the end stages of the disease. I was completely ignorant about other forms of therapy or whether it was possible to treat cancer in any other way but I knew I was on a quest to find out. Little did I know at that time how lonely this quest would turn out to be. As I read, I was feeling hope growing inside of me. Out there in the universe there were others like me who were determined to find a way and, in her book, Dr Turner had identified nine key factors: changing your diet; being responsible for your own health; listening to your intuition; taking herbs and supplements; releasing your past emotional baggage; replacing negative automatic thinking with positive thinking and emotions; finding people or organisations to provide social support; spirituality; and finding a strong reason to live. This book made me feel more composed but I still had no idea how I was going to find someone who would help me to work through this or where I would even begin.

I tried to go through a mental checklist of friends, family and acquaintances with whom I could share this but none sprang immediately to mind. Then as I sat quietly thinking, the voice kicked in again:

"*You need to contact Sally*"

I had struck up a friendship with Sally on the Friday evenings when I attended the Spiritualist Church. Towards the end of my time there, we finished up repeatedly working with each other no matter how we were divided by the use of random card pairing to pick a partner. In the end, our group leader decided that it was a clear indication that we were meant to work together. It was at the time when I was channelling guides and going into trance. Sally too had decided to leave the group as the changes took place. I still had her number in my phone and I gave her a ring asking her if it was possible to meet up. She was a reiki practitioner and was working with both animals and people. I felt I needed to go into deep meditation to get some answers. I also felt that I could talk to her, tell her what was happening for me and that it would be dealt with both in confidence and without judgement.

Meanwhile I received a follow-up from my GP with a copy of the letter that had been sent by the consultant stating clearly that I had been diagnosed with asymptomatic, multifocal breast cancer in the left breast. One tumour had been confirmed as a Grade 2 and the other a Grade 1, both ER positive, HER2 negative. (Grade 1 is a slow-growing tumour with mildly abnormal cells; Grade 2 the cells look less normal and are growing faster; ER positive means they are growing in response to the hormone oestrogen). Cytology from the axilla was benign. My strong family history of breast cancer and my experience regarding my mother led me to state that I did not wish to have any surgery, chemotherapy or radiotherapy but would consider anastrozole or tamoxifen and I had been given some information on this. It was also explained that the standard treatment for my type of cancer was unfortunately mastectomy with the option of reconstruction and that, given the current information regarding the tumours, it was likely that I would have a 5-year survival rate of over 90% and a 10-year survival rate of over 85%. There it was in a nutshell. I booked my appointment with my GP to collect my anastrozole. Once again, any chance of rapport was ruled out. My GP who had known me throughout the birth of my children and early adult life had been retired for some time and this was the second replacement GP for him in a short space of time. She read my notes,

Chapter 5 - Diagnosis

looked at me and then began the dialogue which I really did not want to hear:

"*You should consider your options. My mother had the operation and treatment and she is still alive today.*"

I could not contain myself and found myself retorting:

"*My mother had the operation and the therapy and became an alcoholic and died of depression.*"

With that there was nothing more to be said and I collected my prescription and went to the chemist next door. Because it was expensive medication, they had to order it in and put it on repeat at my request. Before I started it, I read through the side effects, some of which sounded unpleasant, but I didn't find anything too alarming at the time.

The plan at that stage was not to tell my family but with the business in India not taking off the way my husband had planned, the mortgage repayments were up for review as to how these would be paid and later, after a discussion with my older son, my husband suggested that perhaps the only way forward was for me to get a second job! I was already exhausted from the first. It was the typical charity/public sector job where you are paid for working 37.5 hours per week but because of shortage of staff and resources you work many more hours as a volunteer - that is the way these jobs operate and can only keep going all the time they find staff who are prepared to continue with their unpaid volunteering because of being dedicated to the job! I have learnt over my working life that 'dedication to a job' means we will find someone who is vulnerable enough to exploit and get the job done for half the price.

I was as usual in the kitchen preparing the supper as the discussion was taking place between father and older son and I was holding back the tears. I just didn't want to have to discuss anything with them. I wanted to do this my way but once again I was being asked to push myself to extinction with more work. It was exactly this type of situation that had made me want to leave the planet in the first place. Although fresh back from holiday I was already exhausted with everything I had had to face and I also began to feel guilty that I had spent money on a holiday when clearly it should have gone towards the mortgage. With the discussion at an end between father and son, the outcome was presented to me that the answer to the mortgage was in fact for me to take a second job. I returned to the kitchen and stood there silently. My intuitive voice spoke:

"***You have to tell them.***"

So I did. I shall never forget that night. It was like exploding a bomb in the room and was not the way I had wanted to tell the family about my diagnosis, if I was going to tell them at all. I could have saved myself the trouble of cooking. My son was devastated by the news and my husband didn't seem to know what to make of it. Much later, when my husband returned to England permanently, he said that he had no idea how serious it was. He just thought it was like any other disease. I am still somewhat dumbfounded that someone can live in such complete detachment that they do not even register after regular announcements on TV that various celebrities have died from cancer. However, it helps me to understand why there was no major reaction from him and also not to feel hurt by it. Also had he been aware of how serious it was, he might have decided to pack up his belongings earlier to come back from India and 'look after me'. More than anything at this time I needed to be on my own. That might seem strange particularly when everyone advocates group support. But what group would support me? I wasn't doing conventional therapy so I guess this would allocate me to the terminally ill group but I wasn't that either. It was a very desolate path I had chosen because when I felt scared there was no one to tell except my dog, but what she radiated from her eyes was more loving than any comforting words. After some time, my older son, being a scientist and filled with fear that I would die, began to ask me what options I had and why I wasn't doing what they wanted me to do. I understand that he did it out of love and concern but these were exactly the conversations that I had not wanted to have. It wasn't because I was in denial, it was because I could not do what everyone else was doing. Seeing his attitude made me all the more convinced that I wasn't going to share my ill health with others if I could help it. I was becoming stressed and felt as though I was losing the plot; I felt angry that I was being treated like a child who needed someone to make an informed decision for me. I was from the medical world and I knew the score and I had no intention of changing my mind. I explained that I wasn't turning everything down, that I was starting on anastrozole and that was as far as I would go at this time. I just could not listen to what everyone else thought was best for me. I had gone through my share of bullying most of my life but this time I knew I had to stand up for myself and take my own decisions about my life and, if necessary, my death.

CHAPTER 6

On the Road to Recovery

I continued to work and work really hard. Since I wasn't having treatment there was no reason to stop work or to ask for sick time. So I carried on as 'normal'. My nights were disturbed and I would frequently doze off for an hour or so and then wake with that sick feeling and tightness in your gut when you know something is wrong and then in the dark, the stark reality brings you fully awake. I would lie there thinking about how long I might have to live. What things did I need to deal with? The house and garage were particularly a mess but this was not all my possessions. Before my husband left for India, he had filled yet another part of the garage with boxes of glasses, fire extinguishers and pieces of carpet from a failing pub business that he had managed to sell on. It was actually overflowing with everyone's belongings but no one had any time nor the interest to deal with it. The same was true of the house.

I then let my mind drift on to what sort of a funeral I would have. I definitely didn't want a dirge-filled Catholic burial with 'ashes to ashes, dust to dust' stuff. I remember reading the book *Sky Burial* and thought this sounded like a rather natural way to deal with the body, leaving it for the birds of prey particularly given my tendency to fly with an eagle in meditation. The idea of going to Tibet for the final months sounded beautiful - high in the mountains, close to the sky and spirit. I then began to think about Iona and who would look after her. We had become so close. She would sit and wait on the landing for me and the moment she heard my car return she would race down the stairs and be waiting to launch herself at me as soon as I opened the door. At night she would jump on my bed and cuddle up close, particularly as I always felt cold. Such a beautiful loving creature! Later, when the family were around to observe, we realised that even when I came home at different times of the day, she would start to get ready to greet me a good ten minutes before I arrived. I know it was telepathy between us but the family was more sceptical about this though they all agree we were special together! I wouldn't have called myself depressed at this time, more floating in limbo not having anything real to focus on except my job, which did at least take my mind off the reality.

When I caught sight of myself sometimes in the mirror and the bags under my eyes were now becoming so large that I could have used them for shopping, I realised I looked in pretty poor shape! My colleague finally addressed the situation telling me I should go to my doctor as she thought there was something very wrong with me. Reluctantly I told her. We were now down to a two-woman show at work as our other colleague had retired in the earlier part of the year. I had held off saying anything as I did not want her to feel she would have had to change her retirement plans if she had known my situation. So once she retired, I knew it was only fair to tell my other colleague with whom I was working so closely. Her immediate response was that I should tell the boss and go off sick but I explained that I was not ready for this yet. She was shocked when she heard my decision regarding my treatment plan as having looked after another member of staff earlier on to whom she became a Macmillan buddy, she was sure I would need the same. She agreed to abide by what I wanted initially but periodically reminded me that I should think about at least letting our boss know. I didn't really see any reason for this as in no way was my condition detrimental to my work and, apart from sleepless nights, which many in the work population suffer from including my colleague, it was having no adverse effects. If anything, I was more focused than ever before. Also, we did not know what was going to happen to the service. It was major cut-back time with the Tory Government and just as they were busy axing the probation service and giving it out to tender, we had no idea what would happen to us. It was certainly very clear that if it was to have a future it needed more than two people to cover vast areas of Hampshire!

About three months into my course of anastrozole, I began to notice some very scary things were happening. I would get into my car to drive to an appointment and I would forget where I was going and would have to stop and look it up in my diary. One evening I was travelling back on my usual road home that I had travelled for more than twenty years and

Chapter 6 - On the Road to Recovery

I suddenly had no idea where I was. I also found that I would go into a shop to do basic shopping and couldn't remember what I had come in for. The other thing I noticed was my hair was falling out in large quantities and had become incredibly thin. It reminded me of the side effects of chemotherapy but this was not supposed to be chemo, was it? This was 'hormone therapy' supposed to remove the oestrogen from the body and not allow the tumour its fuel supply to grow, but now it seemed to be having remarkably similar side effects to chemotherapy.

By month four, I was now experiencing painful ligaments in the small joints of my hands and feet. It felt like the ligaments were falling apart and my fingers would make clicking sounds as if I had lax ligaments and I was double jointed. I looked inside the packet for the leaflet and discovered that the box did not say Arimidex, which was the usual brand name. It had clearly been changed by the pharmacy following instruction from the GP to a variety which supposedly contained the same ingredient, namely anastrozole, but had a different brand name. I knew from my medical centre days that audits were frequently done by a paid pharmacist to document how many patients were on expensive drugs and who could be changed to a cheaper variety. I knew also that Arimidex is not cheap so clearly, since I was a patient who was likely to die soon, why would you give me an expensive drug? I took the medication back to the GP and explained that the side effects were now getting horrendous as I was having difficulty in walking and this did not happen when I was on Arimidex. She changed it back and as I went into the end of month five of medication, I requested an ultrasound scan of my left breast to check whether there were any real changes happening with this drug. I was very reluctantly given a scan and it did show that both tumours appeared to have shrunk slightly. However, the joint pains continued and I began to despair at the thought of not being able to knit or weave or dance or walk properly again. I now started to feel very depressed.

One morning, Iona began to lick my face and hands requesting her usual morning run. I went to put my feet on the ground and found I could barely hobble to the bathroom. I forced myself to walk with her that morning though the pain was excruciating. Originally, I had tried to convince myself that this was a small price to pay for shrinking the tumours but now I seriously doubted it. Christmas was fast approaching and I tried to turn my mind to everyone coming home and needing to get Christmas meals together. I had good days and bad days with my joints but I continued to walk through the pain and tried not to dwell on it too much. I will never forget that Christmas! The day came and went uneventfully as did Boxing Day until it came to the evening. It was around 9 p.m. and I loaded the dishwasher. As I bent down, suddenly I felt tightness all around my head. It felt as though a metal band was squeezing my head tighter and tighter. I stood up and, for the first time since this had all began, I felt a fear like I have never felt before. I felt as though I was going to have a stroke!

"*Oh my God, what's happening?*" I said out loud.

Luckily the boys were all in the other room watching Christmas TV. Suddenly my intuitive voice began:

"***You need to look at the real side effects, not just what is on the leaflet. Go and see what people are blogging.***"

I went to my laptop and I Googled 'side effects of Arimidex' and it wasn't long before my suspicion was confirmed. There was indeed a link between cardiovascular problems including stroke and I was not the only one out there that was finding similar types of symptoms. I made a vow there and then, shrinkage or no shrinkage, that I was not going to risk a stroke. It was done with. There was no conventional way forward that could help me. If my life was to be shorter and happy with dance, running my dog and walking with her across fields so be it! It was not long after this decision that my intuitive older son asked me if I was still taking the medication, particularly as he had seen the scan results showed that there were positive results. I have never been a good liar and since he confronted me by looking me straight in the eyes, he knew! After a suitable explosion on his behalf, which I fully understood, I explained that I could not tolerate the side effects any longer and in the New Year I would be looking for answers. When I was first diagnosed, he had offered to pay for private surgery and once again he gave me this option along with anything else which might aid my recovery.

At the beginning of January 2015, my husband returned to India again to continue with his business, having been home for a few weeks for Christmas. The boys returned to their respective places and I was glad of this so that I could be alone again to focus only on me. If I were to recover, I had to be completely selfish, living my life entirely for me. I was now coming into year 4 of my job and the burn-out time for such a post was 3 years. I was tired, struggling with the workload and my illness, and there was no way I could have coped with living in a situation where someone relied on me for everything. I began to intuit what I needed to begin the process of recovery until I could take sick leave, which I envisaged as being at the beginning of the new financial year when any

Chapter 6 - On the Road to Recovery

changes at work that were to take place would either be happening or would have happened.

I had begun doing yoga classes but I was finding these increasingly difficult. I found the stretches and strenuous exercises made me feel quite light headed and I would feel slightly strange and uncomfortable. I wished there was a tai chi class in the area but somehow it didn't seem to really gel with people in the same way that yoga does. Once again, past experiences started to surface. Some years before my illness, I had visited Holy Island off the coast of the Aran Isle in Scotland. This beautiful Samye Ling Tibetan Buddhist World Peace Centre with a guest house, a Mandela garden, courses run for yoga, meditation and tai chi throughout the year and scrumptious vegetarian food, called me to it when life had become so difficult on the home front. Ever since visiting the centre, I had been on their emailing system and received regular newsletters. I felt drawn back again as if there was something I needed to put in my life to help me heal myself. I scrolled through the newsletter and found an eight-week beginners' meditation class at their Centre in London. Although I knew how to meditate, I felt I had to begin to learn it properly. I had used guided meditation up until now but never entered into silence and breath meditation. I phoned and signed up and began travelling to Spa Road in London every Wednesday night.

It took a great deal of commitment after work in the cold January nights. I would rush home from work, walk Iona and then take the early evening train. I had no idea why I was really doing this or what I was expecting to find but it was an inexplicable compulsion to go. I was already familiar with temple culture from my time living in India and Bangladesh and on my first night after removing my shoes and socks I entered the shrine room. It was so incredibly beautiful with such a serenity that it seemed hard to believe that we were in the hub of London. The enormous, ornate, gold statue of Buddha dominated the room and then several other aspects of the deity were depicted in picture form around the room. I am not Buddhist nor do I profess to be any particular religion as I prefer to keep my mind open and explore. By the age of 13, I had been dabbling in other religions and certainly Buddhism had captured my imagination after coming across the picture in the school library of monks sitting in the mountain snows of Tibet. It didn't, however, capture my mother's imagination when she found out that not only was I blasphemous but I had also dared to enter a dirty public library and borrow books that would give me even further knowledge about other religions. She took every opportunity she could to return them to the public library where they very definitely belonged, for heathens. This, however, did not stop my compulsion to explore and, once I left home, I was reading even more avidly. I think what drew me to Buddhism the most was the development of the self and the concept of reincarnation. When I studied genetics in biology, albeit at a basic level, I would wonder what would be the point of living if only your genetic make-up was passed on to the next generation but not all your experiences. Why, in fact, were we going through all this 'life experience' if it was to finish in a grave of ashes at the end of it all? You would only ever impart a small portion of your experiences to your children but what happened to every single person's individual experiences that had ever lived on the earth plane. It became a little mind-blowing by the age of 15 but I did wonder about past lives as a possibility of growing these experiences and thoughts and passing them on.

The first two weeks of meditation were hard – just even sitting still as I was now beginning to realise that the concept that my condition had been 'asymptomatic' was far from true. My whole body had been crying out for years that it was getting into difficulties but I had not been listening, until after my diagnosis when I finally looked in the mirror and saw in the reflection that looked back at me that I was in fact dying. So not only had I not been 'listening', I had not been 'seeing' either. This word 'LISTEN' was to be presented to me later during my therapy and became such an important word. So, as I sat for the first time in the stillness, I realised that one of the symptoms had been pain in sitting, especially when driving. I found that after 20 minutes of driving, my left leg in particular would start to seize up and I needed to stop the car, get out and move around. I now know that the gall bladder meridian runs down the outside of the leg and one of the acupuncture points (GB30) lies deep under the gluteal muscles). Stagnant energy in the breast area is linked to the gall bladder meridian. In Chinese medicine, the gall bladder is also associated with the emotion of anxiety. Similarly, the bladder meridian also runs through the gluteal region. It regulates the autonomic nervous system responsible for fight and flight. My body had definitely been trying to indicate to me that the stress levels were out of control. The stress was not only being held in the abdominal area where I normally held it, but in other parts of my body and ultimately in the organs too. If I had told a Western doctor that I had pain and stiffness in the left buttock and this was a symptom of breast cancer, they would probably have decided that I was completely nuts, but looking back I had had this symptom for years and sitting for long periods was very

Chapter 6 - On the Road to Recovery

problematic. Another symptom was how cold my hands and feet were over the years and how I could not warm my body, again a symptom of a poorly oxygenated body and a depletion of the life force. I had also had an itchy left breast which flared up from time to time but I had ignored it. A peculiar thing was happening as I became more unwell. Everything was starting to taste of salt, particularly when I ate something sweet and my strong sense of smell had diminished. But perhaps the most important sign of all was the stabbing pains in the kidney areas just where the adrenal glands sit. I used to drive to work in the morning and frequently pull in at a lay-by as shooting, darting, spasmodic waves of pain would almost take my breath away. I was in an adrenal crisis from the stress of life but I had no idea what it was. Prolonged stress, whether as a result of emotional, environmental or physical factors, is disastrous for the adrenals. Eventually, progesterone in a woman may be diverted to the adrenals to support the production of cortisol which is falling off because the adrenals can no longer manufacture it. This leaves the body in a situation of oestrogen dominance. Oestrogen is what fires a breast tumour if it is oestrogen positive!

In order to meditate on silence, we focused our minds on the sounds in the room. I became acutely aware of the sounds coming from the radiator, the sounds of traffic outside and then gradually the stillness that was being created in the room by over eighty people. It made me realise how much noise we live with on a daily basis and I have since become aware of the 'noise' created by all the technological interference. I wonder at the animals and plants around us in nature being able to adapt to such a huge interference in their habitat but maybe they are not really adapting and showing us this by becoming sick as a warning to us.

Gradually, I made friends with some of the regulars and as the weeks went by, the enthusiastic eighty or more congregation dwindled to around twenty-five. I felt a special affinity for a woman called Linda who very kindly dropped me at the Tube station on those winter nights and it was not long before we realised why we had a common bond with similarities from childhood that followed through into adulthood. She too was studying hypnotherapy with a special interest in regression therapy. She was also a reiki practitioner. We gradually became good friends and now meet up once a year for Premal & Miten concerts in London along with a meal and a catch up. We feel we have known each other for ever and I am sure we have! It was about the fifth or sixth session when Linda sat beside me. Normally she sat on the cushions cross-legged on the floor but I found the chairs at the back of the room more comfortable because of my sitting difficulty. We were again sitting meditating quietly on the breath when I felt an enormous surge and an out-of-body experience taking over me and I could see a deity-like figure in front of me, glowing in gold and shades of pinks and blues. At first, I did not know what deity it was and I tried to search in my mind through the various gods and goddesses I had seen in the many Hindu temples I had visited in my travels through India. Then a 'knowing' that it was Vishnu came through loud and clear. He was surrounded in golden light and from his hands came showers of gold coins. I had no idea what this meant and the vibration of energy through my body was phenomenal. I do not know in reality how long this lasted because, in meditation, real time is generally lost to us but I recall gradually being brought back into the room by the sound of the Tibetan singing bowl. My friend next to me looked at me and said:

"*What was that?*"

She had clearly felt the surge of energy while sitting beside me. I tried to explain what I had seen and experienced but since I had no real idea what it was all about, it was difficult to explain to someone else without coming across as some sort of a religious convert. Two years after this event, I asked Linda if she could recall that night and she texted me back with the following:

"*I recall being drawn to you, I cannot say why. I would always happily sit on the floor but that day I felt drawn to sit next to you. When the meditation started, it was different from any other one I had done, I immediately had colour all around me. From memory it was pink and green light. I then felt a pulling towards the ceiling and I was conscious of you being next to me and rising upwards. You said afterwards you were on the ceiling for the whole meditation looking down. I was open to light travelling through my body. I honestly think we were both off piste as I'm sure we were being guided but both did our own thing!*"

Later, I explored more about this deity, who in Hinduism represents the preserver and restorer, and his female deity, Lakshmi, who is the goddess of wealth. Both are associated with abundance and clearly the showering of gold coins was another way of expressing this. Well, I was definitely in need of abundance at that time. I knew I was going to have to go off sick at some stage in order to address how I was going to 'heal' myself. I would, if I was lucky, be entitled to perhaps four months' sick leave but I was not really sure. Would I be entitled to this if I was not following conventional therapy? I didn't know. My visionary encounter had certainly been a very beautiful, comforting experience and an input of very high vibrations into my body but I did not really understand and

Chapter 6 - On the Road to Recovery

still don't today fully understand the significance of it. The more I study the concepts behind the ancient scriptures, the more I realise that these are not 'religious' concepts as we know them to be in the Christian sense. On reflection, I feel that it was presented to me as a visual of a higher source of energy, particularly in the form of pink, which I associate with unconditional love, and gold, which has such purity about it. The coins to me represented that if I channelled my energy to the higher realms then I would find everything I needed there. The secret also was somewhere in these breathing techniques and silence.

I continued to attend my eight-week course of meditation and my friendship with Linda grew ever more comfortable and beautiful to the point where I was able to tell her what was going on for me. Like Sally, she did not judge, she did not say that my path was doomed for disaster, she just accepted. The Tibetan Centre was to play an even more important role in my recovery a few weeks later but for now I was back into meditation again, I was becoming calmer and more accepting of the path I had chosen. The waking in the night thinking my death was imminent began to diminish and I was sleeping much more soundly. Because there was no one else at home except my dog, it gave me the opportunity to sleep at 10 pm or earlier if I wished. All the years of sleep deprivation I had undergone were gradually being replenished and I was definitely entering into a more peaceful phase of my life.

At the same time as finding the meditation class, I was being guided to another answer to my symptoms that occurred from the anastrozole. Since I had stopped taking it, my head symptoms had not recurred but my small joints were still bothering me. Since the book *Radical Remission* had guided me so far, in despair one day I asked if there was something I was missing and I just allowed the book to open. It opened at Chapter 6, page 185, and there was an account of a woman who was using Tibetan herbs. Did my Tibetan Centre also know of a Tibetan doctor who might be able to help me at least with these awful symptoms? I had begun my meditation class on 14th January 2015 and there on the notice board was an advertisement for Dr Soktsang, a trained Tibetan Medicine practitioner, with over thirty years' experience in Tibet, India and the UK. He had also trained in Dharamshala, India!! Again, I felt I was being guided. On 18th January 2015, I attended my first appointment with Dr Soktsang. He spoke very little English but it didn't seem to really matter as he was more interested in what my pulses were doing and what my tongue looked like. He described how he would send me some herbs from the Tara Centre in Scotland and they would be in powder form and three separate bags of crushed herbs which were to be taken three times a day. I have no idea what these herbs were and to this day still have no idea. All I know is that one week after taking them my joints stopped clicking and I began to feel some sort of vitality return to my body. I am sure there are many sceptics that would like to believe that this was a placebo effect but since taking the herbs I have had no further joint pains in my hands and feet.

Along with my meditation, I was also seeing Sally regularly for reiki. This was invaluable as, with her energy vibrations and my own, I was going ever deeper into meditation. By doing this, I was getting in tune with my own body and there were times when I received direct 'messages' in either auditory or visual forms of the type of food I needed to eat. Before my diagnosis, I had experienced a craving for fish. This seemed very odd to me since I had been vegetarian for many years but it became so intense that eventually I gave way to it and found myself eating salmon or tuna at least twice a week. Under Sally's care, I was instructed about the importance of my diet when in deep meditation since up until that time I had not bothered about my body at all. In the stillness, I listened and took note of the visuals of leafy green vegetables I was being shown. 'Let food be thy medicine and medicine thy food' from Hippocrates, the father of medicine, sums it up very nicely. My diet over the years had been at least four bars of chocolate a day! Starting with a Mars bar for breakfast and followed by bags of Maltesers, Milky Bars and an assortment of milk chocolate and crisps during the day. I could eat my way through a packet of chocolate biscuits in a matter of an hour, particularly when I was running from one job to another. A lot of my work involved meeting clients, attending courts and meetings and it was easier to snack on junk than pack a decent lunch. That took time and effort! When I was living alone, I rarely took any fresh fruit or vegetables. A banana was about the sum total of my 5 a day. By evening, when I returned home tired and drained, I would wash the junk food down with a glass of red wine and if it had been a particularly stressful day then sometimes two. I had noticed that over a period of two years I had jumped a dress size from 12 to 14 and my body felt overweight and lethargic. I had remembered reading that once you reached middle age, putting on those extra pounds could put you at an increased risk of breast cancer. But caring for myself was not really in my remit and, because I had never had any major illness in my life, I thought I was invincible.

CHAPTER 7

The Importance of Diet and Exercise

I had already been given an important clue by my body with regards to my diet when it began craving fish at least six months before diagnosis. This was to be the beginning of many curious cravings similar to those experienced in pregnancy. The body is truly remarkable in saying what it needs. Salmon, I later learnt provides important amounts of the antioxidant amino acid taurine. It is known to have antioxidant and anti-inflammatory effects on the body and in addition studies have shown that it can cause apoptosis in cancer cells. Apoptosis comes from the ancient Greek for 'falling off' and is a process where cell death is programmed in an organism if the organism is under threat. Not only this but salmon is a source of vitamin B12, vitamin D and selenium and a source of niacin, omega-3 fatty acids, protein, phosphorus and vitamin B6. It is also a good source of choline (needed to help maintain cell membranes), pantothenic acid or vitamin B5 (which creates red blood cells vital for carrying oxygen around the body), biotin (also needed for the immune system) and potassium (vital in preventing strokes, heart and kidney disorders). This all began to make so much sense so I continually asked my body what it needed. Following a meditation session with Sally, I began to crave spinach. I researched the need for these vegetables and I also learnt the importance of eating organic. The body had enough to deal with in cancer, let alone pesticides and poorly grown food lacking in all sorts of nutrients due to mass production. So I learnt and nourished. I learnt also to cook my vegetables in the best way to preserve the nutrients so when I didn't eat raw, I steamed the spinach. I ate basic foods as we had done as children. So I would bake the salmon in the oven with no added oil, I boiled potatoes in their jackets and steamed vegetables such as spinach, asparagus, broccoli and cauliflower. The more I learnt, the more I removed all processed food from my diet. I would make soda bread, which uses bicarbonate of soda and no sugar.

The further I investigated, the more I realised that the real addictive poison that had been introduced more and more into our diet was sugar. It is in everything. Read the back of the ready-made meals, look at all the processed foods from soup to tomato ketchup - it is in ABSOLUTELY EVERYTHING. If you cleared the supermarket aisles tomorrow of the products that contain sugar you would be left with about two aisles. The food companies are feeding cancer. They keep people ignorant and addicted so that they can go on making a profit. I am shocked when I go into my local petrol station to see aisle after aisle stacked with nothing but products containing sugar. The coffee that we buy in Costa and Starbucks is full of added sugar to give assorted exotic flavours and then finished off by topping it with lashings of cream to pack the calories on. To add insult to injury, the general public are then encouraged to go on healthy eating programmes and exercise campaigns. Sugar needs to be targeted in the same way as cigarettes and made to be as antisocial to consume as smoking. I remember when people smoked in offices and the air was like a dense fog around them. There was no mention of health and safety back then when the whole office could have gone up in smoke if the paperwork had caught fire. But by putting bans on it in public places and sending people outside to smoke, there has gradually been a decline in smoking because it has become antisocial.

In studies in rats, sugar has been shown to activate the brain's pleasure centres more than cocaine. It also provokes cravings and withdrawal symptoms in the same way as drugs. If an attempt were made today for it to be passed as a legal high it would be banned and yet so many people are not aware of this. And not only that - it feeds cancer cells!

I have in the course of my research found another very interesting fact. There has been some research done on the link between fungal infections and cancer. Interestingly, for years I battled with fungal nail infections, particularly of both big toes. In Chinese medicine the great toes are linked with the liver. If the liver were to be paid for its work it would be priceless; if the liver is not functioning well then it is not surprising that the body begins to fail. Recently research has shown that patients going through chemotherapy and radiotherapy frequently have

Chapter 7 - The Importance of Diet and Exercise

fungal nail infections. This makes me wonder if the nail infections were always there, linked to the cancer, but once the chemo and radiotherapy destroys the immune system it allows the fungus to rapidly multiply. I am curious about this link as I think back to my nursing days when, in the 1970s, the answer to a gastric ulcer was to remove all or part of the stomach since the cause was unknown. Miraculously, it was discovered that Helicobacter pylori was responsible and very quickly a triple therapy was researched and given consecutively over 7 to 14 days which now has revolutionised the treatment of gastric ulcers. It may be speculation on my behalf but I remain inquisitive about this link to a sugary environment, coupled with the growth of fungus and cancer.

To return to the topic of diet, today's medical students study one or two weeks of nutrition in the whole of their training. The film *First Do No Harm*, starring Meryl Streep as Lori, tells the story of a boy with epilepsy cured by the ketogenic diet but only after having gone through every drug known to the medical world and finally being offered life-threatening surgery. Lori literally had to abduct her child to get the necessary care - the diet. Just as diet proved to be effective in epilepsy, the same is true with cancer. Cancer Research UK has suggested that added sugar found in fizzy drinks, sweets, cakes and biscuits are best kept as 'treats'. But Cancer Research UK and Macmillan have coffee mornings showing cupcakes being baked to raise funds and, following chemotherapy sessions, people are given ice cream or a cup of tea and a biscuit. So in through the veins we give chemo (which carries a warning to say that it is carcinogenic) and in through the mouth we give another cancer-promoting substance.

In February 2015 I had an appointment with a Macmillan nurse at my local surgery. She had just completed a new course. She was extremely pleasant and spoke to me for a short while regarding diet and what constituted a good nourishing diet. What surprised me was that at no stage was it suggested that sugar be excluded from the diet, that a high intake of fresh fruit and vegetables, preferably organic, be made a number one priority, and that dairy be reduced or stopped. As an ex nurse I began to understand why a drink of radioactive glucose is given to a patient prior to a PET scan to highlight the cancer hotspots. So why weren't other members of the medical profession making these same observations? If radioactive glucose, i.e. sugar, was highlighting cancer cells, this meant that cancer cells had a preference for sugar, not only a preference but actually used it to proliferate. I had a brief discussion with the nurse who thought I was doing fine with my diet and said I probably knew more about it than her! This shocked me, since I did not feel knowledgeable at all at this stage. I was only just beginning to learn and understand the importance of diet and yet the medical professionals appeared to have no knowledge and understanding of cutting all sugar, alcohol and processed food from the diet. Yet it was there on the internet with Chris Woollams on his 'Cancer Active' site and Ty Bollinger in 'Cancer a Global Quest'. I think Hippocrates would definitely not have been impressed by the lack of advancement in the medical profession.

As I left my appointment, I knew I was now flying solo on a journey to find as many answers as I could to work with this disease in a way that did not require mutilation. Sadly, this answer would not lie with modern medicine. Every spare moment I had, I researched diet. Intuitively I thought about fasting. I wondered what effect it would have on cancer cells if I had periods of fasting. So once a month, at the weekend, I went on a fast, having only water with fresh lemon added and herbal teas such as ginger and peppermint. I now make fresh ginger tea using root ginger and grow my own herbs so that I can make fresh tea rather than using commercial tea bags. My body felt better for the fasting and eventually I extended it to two consecutive days so that it would be more effective. I noticed how clear my skin was becoming and that my eyes were brighter and the weight I had put on through unhealthy eating, particularly in my job, began to drop away.

The National Institute on Aging has also studied one type of breast cancer in detail to further understand the effects of fasting on cancer. In their study, during fasting, the cancer cells tried to make new proteins and took other steps to keep growing and dividing. As a result of these steps, which in turn led to a number of other steps, damaging free radical molecules were created which broke down the cancer cells' own DNA and caused their destruction, a form of cellular suicide. The cancer cell is trying to replace all of the stuff missing in the bloodstream that it needs to survive after a period of fasting, but can't. In turn, it tries to create them and this leads to its own destruction. So maybe the idea of fasting in the religious communities long ago was not so much for punishment but for a purification of the body to give it time to cleanse and clear the system.

This led me back to looking at the effects of harmful food in the body and there I came across the importance of an alkaline body rather than acid which is produced when the diet is rich in sugar and carbohydrates. I bought some simple pH sticks from the internet that can tell from your urine whether the body is acid or alkaline. I was shocked when I first

Chapter 7 - The Importance of Diet and Exercise

started using them to see how high a level of acidity my urine was reading and how it varied throughout the day. I then began the day starting with a couple of glasses of fresh water with lemon in. Throughout the day I ate good food including avocado in salads, watercress and slightly green bananas, which I love. I continued to monitor the pH of my urine and it made a remarkable difference to it depending on the foods I ate. After a while my body began to train itself so that I could actually tell before testing whether it was becoming more acidic. If I woke in the morning and the pH was more acidic, I actually knew beforehand because I felt less well in myself. Another interesting aspect was my bowel movements. Prior to diagnosis, and given the diet I was eating, it was not unusual to not have a bowel movement for three days. If I was anxious or having a particularly stressful time and the sugar fix to cope with this was excessive, generally in the form of chocolate, then it was not unusual to suffer from irritable bowel syndrome (IBS). My abdominal area felt permanently bloated and of all the cancers I thought might come my way it would have surprised me less if I had been diagnosed with colon cancer. As I became more observant about the workings of my body, I noticed the changes such as my urine having a different smell when I was eating and drinking nourishing things. My intake of alcohol by this time had been reduced to only having a glass of red wine when I went out socially and the less I consumed of it, the less I desired it.

I also took myself off all dairy products particularly after investigating an article about the low incidence of breast cancer in Chinese village women. They not only don't consume dairy products but actually say, in a derogatory way, that Western people smell of cheese. In the large towns and cities in China, where Western influence is now penetrating, the coffee shops with their huge helpings of cream on top of the coffee and cream cakes are becoming normal. With it, the low rates of breast cancer are disappearing. Of course, you could become obsessive about these things. There are also adverse things being said about soya so I changed to almond milk. I certainly felt after several weeks that my breasts were less tight and Sally too did the same thing and made the same observation. We are the only mammal that consumes another mammal's milk – and such a huge animal in comparison with ourselves. From data collected from a range of research carried out on whether the presence of steroid hormones in dairy products could be counted as having an important risk factor for various cancers in humans it was found that it was in fact significant. I decided that it was time to remove it from my diet. Along with chocolate, I had loved cream – even having single cream added to my milk on a bowl of Rice Krispies was my idea of a delicious breakfast. I also loved trifle and could happily eat a bowlful to start the day! I have now changed my breakfast to a bowl of organic porridge cooked in water and I then add blueberries, pumpkin seeds, walnuts, chia seeds and occasionally a few sultanas and top it with some almond milk. I used to love my coffee but have reduced it down to one cup a day at breakfast, again using almond milk. To help cut my craving for sweet things, I made myself blueberry muffins with stevia for sweetening and used part organic flower with flaxseeds. Flaxseeds again have anti-cancer properties. I changed from milk chocolate to good quality dark chocolate. Since I had always disliked dark chocolate, I thought this would put an end to my cravings but it didn't and so in the end I had to dispense with chocolate completely as my mental craving for it was so great that it had to be axed completely. I won't pretend I don't still struggle with it to this day and I do have special occasion days. If you are too severe on yourself it is like going on a diet. The moment you tell yourself you are on a diet, then of course psychologically you feel that you can't have something and then you crave it even more!

Another important aspect of my diet was the introduction of herbs and supplements. My herbs started with my Tibetan ones but then progressed on to supplements by a very unusual contact. It was suggested by a close friend that, if possible, I should try to have an appointment with two people who were coming to London from the States, Foster Perry and Kristos Tsompanelis, who work together as part of the Golden Hummingbird. One is a shaman and the other a seer. Once I had the link, I booked an appointment for 3rd June 2015. It was worth every penny of the appointment. Kristos was indeed a phenomenal seer and could recount all the important events of my life and told me that I had had cancer on three other occasions but had chosen to bring my body through. He knew me better than I knew myself; I knew exactly what occasions he was referring to but he was recounting them for me loud and clear. From his personal experience of ill health, he made some very valuable suggestions as to how I could start to rebuild my immune system. He suggested Wobenzym N, which is a combination of plant-derived enzymes bromelain and papain and other enzymes that supposedly support a healthy immune system. He suggested BioBran MGN3, made from breaking down rice bran with enzymes from the Shitake mushrooms, and used to stimulate a weak immune system, particularly in the case of a body with cancer. I was also recommended Essiac tea, a tea made from Sheep Sorrel, Burdock Root, Slippery Elm

Chapter 7 - The Importance of Diet and Exercise

Bark and Turkish Rhubarb. The first two herbs have adverse effects on cancer cells and the latter two again build the immune system. He also explained to me about juicing, green juicing in particular, and the importance of raspberry extracts and berries. Again, he reiterated a raw diet, preferably vegan, especially possible during the summer months, and to look at food websites, such as Russell James to get ideas for food preparation. Alcohol and sugar should be removed from the diet completely. Without me telling him what I had discovered already, he was reinforcing for me the need to strengthen the immune system. However, he told me the most important thing for my recovery was to abandon the past. Let go of everything that had led me into thinking I could not fulfil my life. He gave me some clues as to where this might lie and mentioned energy work, astrology, healing spaces, sacred geometry, meditation, shamanism and creative design. Every one of these as he said them really resonated in my body and made me feel excited and alive. They had, in fact, been what I had been slowly pursuing all my life but had not yet reached fruition. When I left them both that day, I felt a sense of hope. My work was now to build my immune system and pursue my dreams. How I was going to do the latter I didn't have a clue but I was offered something solid that now I could work with. Kristos as an astrologer had told me that 2015 was an extremely important year for me and that there are certain years that are turning points. My next big one would be 2023. I looked at him and asked him if he thought I would be still alive for that one and he didn't reply. He knew like me that there would be one hell of a lot of hurdles to jump over on the way - most of all, the conditioning we take on board throughout our lives.

The other big love of my life and hugely important in my recovery was dance. Before I went on my holiday trek in Peru, I had been attending the local sports centre to do dance workouts to increase my fitness. Since the idea of sweating it out on a bicycle or rowing machine was not for me and I had already got a membership going, I was attending three dance classes a week. I attended every Tuesday and Wednesday night and Sunday morning, rarely missing a class. Nikki and Jade, a mum and daughter team, were my two instructors and one particular song in Jade's class that she finished the session with was 'The Zumbe, Zumbe Song'. I would pound the floor with this and my love for dance together with the need to put a growing strength back into my body and Jade's inspirational choreography gave me a new lease of life. I began to think:

"I can't be that ill if at the ripe old age of sixty I can move around the floor like this with twenty- and thirty-year-olds."

Eventually, after a session where my friend and I got the wrong end of the stick when Jade said she wouldn't be doing the sessions, I blurted out what her sessions meant to me. Fortunately, Jade was not leaving but just taking some leave. When she knew what the 'Zumbe, Zumbe' song meant to me she played it frequently and gave me a knowing smile. However, we had to be careful not to bore the socks off of everyone else in the class! She still plays it today for variety and it still continues to uplift me because I now know that I can't be that sick if I can work three hours of full-on aerobic exercise per week, plus run with my dog for a mile every morning and walk with her for over an hour every day. Above all, dance makes my heart sing and the energy it produces in a room full of like-minded people is phenomenal. Unfortunately, one of the young GPs at my local surgery was not of the same opinion as me. When I finally went off sick in April 2015 to take care of myself and listen to my body's needs, I was told that if I could dance, I was well enough to go back to work. To be fair, how could you expect someone of that age to understand that you were eating, resting and dancing your way back to health after years of stress, overwork and not caring for yourself? I had been working since I was 15 years old, had rarely had a day off work, and had never had a certificate for ill health; but because I had not had surgery, chemo or radiotherapy, why should I need to take time off? That was the last time I tried to explain the truth of what I was trying to do.

CHAPTER 8

The Haven

Breast Cancer Haven is very appropriately named. As I approached it on a cold winter's day, it gave off an air of warmth even from the outside. I felt like a weary traveller finding a place of safety and protection to rest and retreat for a while from the outside world. It is summed up very aptly on the 'Cancer Active' website when they say "Walking into Breast Cancer Haven in London is a little like taking a long cool drink when you are very thirsty on a hot day, or finally sitting down in front of a fire with a cup of tea at the end of a long, chilly journey home from work." It is a beautiful converted church, so most probably sitting on a ley line and the energy around and in it is phenomenal. The church windows emit light from all aspects of the building and this is what awaits you when you enter – pure light! As you come in through the heavy wooden doors, you see a striking, round, modern stained-glass window straight in front of you, just above the seating area. Plants abound and there is a small library containing anything from books on dietary advice and cookery books to spiritual aspects of healing, visualisation, yoga and meditation. To the right of the entrance is the reception desk and I do not know how the Haven Reception staff are selected but it would be very helpful if NHS reception staff were sent even for one day of shadowing these lovely people. Such a warmth and caring exudes from them from the moment you arrive into the centre. Nothing is too much trouble and everyone who comes to the Haven is referred to as a 'visitor' – not a 'patient' nor 'client' but a 'visitor' implying that you are a guest and afforded – well, above all, the word 'respect' springs to mind. How very different from my GP and hospital experience – so cold, frightening and uncaring, particularly from the senior professionals. I appreciate that the NHS, because of the sheer volume of patients they have to see, cannot give the same personal touch. But kindness, warmth and particularly eye contact, costs nothing as you go about your daily work.

I had come for the Haven Introduction Day so that I could get a flavour of what they offered in the way of programmes, and to meet the staff and other visitors going through similar experiences. There were seven other visitors with me and we were taken upstairs to a room which, once again, had a stunning, round stained-glass window and the low winter sun was filtering through in red, orange, blue, yellow, pink and white light, cut in the shapes of circles and flowers. It reminded me of the chakras of the body and a perfect spiritual place to recover. However, apart from my surroundings, I do not remember a great deal of that day because as we did our personal introductions, I realised that even here in such calming surroundings I felt that I did not belong. As we took it in turns, each person related their particular cancer journey so far, which for the most part included surgery, chemotherapy and radiotherapy followed by hormone treatment. I also noticed some were wearing head scarves or talked about having purchased a wig and how awful they found this to wear. We were not talking in order around the room, so I had time to digest that I was completely alone on my particular journey. No one had refused conventional treatment. The closest person to my situation was someone who had had their breast lump removed and was deciding that probably they would refuse anymore treatment but were unsure at this stage. I waited until last, introduced myself and stated that I was searching for a way forward other than the usual treatment offered. There was a hush in the room and I could sense the group's astonishment so I quickly cut short my story. I wondered if I had made a big mistake. Would I be denied any help because I was not really a true cancer patient? On my particular journey, I realised that SILENCE was to be my friend and my best way forward. When we had a break before the next session, several of the ladies told me they thought I was very brave, that they couldn't do what I was doing. I couldn't bring myself to say to them that I was too afraid to do what they were doing because it horrified me.

The time had come to listen quietly and as the day progressed, we were given plenty of information on good diet, and the preparation of simple, sugar-free, nutritious meals. However, once again I felt odd as it was explained that protein intake and following a dairy-free diet for a vegetarian would pose some additional difficulties. I appeared to be the

Chapter 8 - The Haven

only vegetarian in the room because when we were asked if anyone was vegetarian, no one else volunteered that they were, so I didn't either. However, when we went for lunch in the café in the basement, there was the most delicious vegetarian food waiting for us. I am sure it had taken a lot of preparation by the two ladies serving it and trying to prepare such food on a daily basis would be very time consuming particularly when working.

After lunch, relaxation, meditation and exercise were discussed. Gentle exercise such as walking 15 to 30 minutes per day to avoid over exerting the body in the early stages of recovery was recommended. Nordic walking, yoga and Qigong were also suggested. How could I explain that I had a mad Irish Setter who liked to run on a lead with me for 30 minutes in the morning and take me hiking across fields of mud for over an hour in the evenings. Not to mention Zumba classes three times a week. These two activities were another reason why I didn't want to have surgery. If some of my lymph nodes under my arm had been excised, this could have caused lymphoedema and would have affected my strength to hold my very energetic dog on lead and to raise my left arm above my head in an exercise class. I enjoyed my day at the Haven but I left in the evening feeling like a complete freak. What was the matter with me? Why didn't I just go and do what everyone else was doing, confront it and learn to live with it all like my mother had done. Accept it as my genetic predisposition and move on. As I made my way to the underground station, I felt really low although something told me that I needed to go back to the Haven again - but for what, I didn't know.

When I got home, I decided I would phone the Haven the next day and see if I would be eligible for the 10 free sessions of my choice to be discussed when meeting with the cancer information manager. When I called it was suggested I meet with Sonia, who would gather my information and then talk me through the options. An appointment was made for the next week; we were now in mid-November 2015 - one and a half years since my cancer diagnosis. Apart from feeling really tired particularly early morning and evening I had no other real symptoms. My meeting with Sonia was memorable. She couldn't have been lovelier. She was a lively lady with a good sense of humour, and we chatted through my options. I didn't mind when she said that she had to, of course, point out to me that she would recommend the conventional treatment for cancer but at no stage did she force this opinion on me or suggest that there was nothing they could offer me at the Haven because of my decision. A programme was drawn up for me and my next appointment was to see Edem about welfare benefits and money advice. I was fast coming to the end of my sick time and pay and was looking to go gradually back to work part time, but had no desire to do so at this point because physically I tired so easily.

Edem was a wealth of information on finances, talking me through possible tax rebates, looking at any small pensions that could be cashed in and whether I was entitled to any benefits. Above all she claimed a Macmillan grant for me which covered a NutriBullet to make up fresh smoothies and fresh vegetable soups for myself. I could not have afforded this without the grant and my old Braun blender was sadly in no fit condition for the job. In addition, she claimed for clothing for me as I had now dropped from a size 14 to size 10 thanks to my new healthy lifestyle of eating well and exercising. My smart work trousers hung off my body and even though I had tried moving the waist button this then displaced the zip so no matter how I tried to make them work they would have needed radical alteration in only the way a tailor sitting in the market places of India would know how to do cheaply and efficiently. My casual trousers were the same but I could manage with a belt around them and a baggy sweater over the top. My greatest need was a laptop. I no longer had one since I had given this up when the job had been TUPE-ed and my eight-year-old PC no longer appeared to have any life left in it, not even turning on anymore. Without this, I was cut off from investigating how to progress any further with my journey. When my grant arrived (very promptly) I decided my priority was the NutriBullet, which I got in a Christmas sale for half price. I bought a pair of smart trousers in my new size. At last I was the size I had always wanted to be – a trim size 10 with no waist fat anymore over the waistband. I looked at myself ruefully in the mirror feeling that it was a pity I had had to become so ill before I decided to sort my body out. When my eldest son arrived from America, he looked for laptops and, having selected a good model, he suggested I wait until Boxing Day as it was to be discounted by £200. For me it was far more important now to connect with the outside world rather than use the rest of my grant to buy better fitting clothes. My laptop changed my life once I purchased it. I could now look at what other people were doing, follow the Cancer Active website with all the new innovative ways forward that Chris Woollams is so good at putting together. I was also able to play my Premal & Miten CDs and open up my spiritual world again.

Chapter 8 - The Haven

The Haven was becoming my sanctuary. My next session was with Julie, the nutritional therapist. I had two sessions with her over a period of several weeks as she talked me through my diet and monitored it. Although I thought I had been doing well with diet, she pointed out that it might be the Christmas Season but mince pies were definitely not part of the 'cancer diet'! We worked with starting the day with a hearty porridge breakfast with the addition of chia seeds, pumpkin seeds, walnuts full of selenium, and blueberries. I like porridge cooked in water only and then to cool it I applied some almond milk. I also allowed myself one cup of coffee per day and acquired a taste for almond milk in it as I am not a fan of black coffee. During my travels through Greece I had learnt to love Mediterranean vegetables and a really easy dish is to fill an oven proof dish with organic onions, red, green and yellow peppers, plum tomatoes, mushrooms, pine seeds, dried herbs, courgettes, olives and a sprinkling of olive oil and into the oven for approximately half an hour to bake at 200 degrees C. For additional protein, I add a small amount of halloumi and let it melt and give up its salt into the vegetables for the last 10 minutes and accompany this with couscous. Such a simple meal but it is 'eating the rainbow' as Chris Woollams suggests on his 'Cancer Active' website, and therefore contains all the nutrients you could need in such a delicious meal. Very occasionally I would allow myself to have a glass of good quality red wine to go with it, though alcohol is not recommended by the Haven. With the help of Julie, we worked on reducing my cravings for chocolate by initially changing to dark chocolate but in its purest form. However, it still continued to be my Achilles heel so I knew that chocolate needed to go because until that went, my mental and physical need for sugar would never be over. I was given a booklet on healthy eating and I purchased their cookbook for further ideas. I wondered why none of this was done in group sessions in GP surgeries by the Macmillan nurses employed there. Diet was still not being seen as one of the key factors in restoring the immune system and ultimately the body, particularly where this disease was concerned.

With my diet now sorted, it was time to turn to the knots of stress in my body which I didn't need a massage to tell me was sitting in lumps in my shoulders and neck. We have such illuminating expressions in the English language for what is going on - 'She is carrying the weight of the world on her shoulders' or 'He is a pain in the neck'. And as we say it, so it becomes. Denise was to be my next port of call and after one hour of really good upper body massage I felt a lot lighter. I had not had such a good massage since my brother had used me for a practice model when he was training and learning all the muscles of the body. How many moons ago that now seemed. As Denise worked with me, particularly on my back, shoulders and neck, I discussed with her how deep I felt the stress had gone and that I didn't really know what would release all of it. She suggested sessions of acupuncture with Christopher. I lay thinking about this. I was not sure that I wanted little needles poking out of me, nor did I want a male therapist. Up until now all my therapists had been female and apart from my brother's gentle male energy, I had not really encountered it in the males that I lived or worked with. I had booked a few more massage sessions but Denise suggested that if I wanted to change my sessions I could, by meeting with Sonia again and discussing this with her.

Just before Christmas, I had two sessions of Mind/Body booked with Gosia. She describes herself as a transformational coach and speaker and is also now the author of *The Expansion Game*. As we made a cup of tea together downstairs, I was aware of her energy and no doubt she was tuning into mine. Once we were in her treatment room, she said something which took me by surprise.

"*You are a very powerful woman.*"

I wasn't really sure what she meant.

"*You have so many things you can do.*"

Well, certainly I had a wealth of careers behind me, none of which I particularly wanted to do, nor had I stayed long enough in any to excel. I mulled this over and then she began asking about the more personal issues in my life and since I had already been exploring the root cause of my ill health it was easy to discuss it openly with her. Gosia was aware that I did not want to change my decision on conventional treatment and so worked with me at this level. She helped me to release old patterns of behaviour in a humorous way by making it seem ridiculous what you were looking forward to in life by choosing old patterns of conditioned behaviour. It was the first time that someone validated with me what I already knew; my thinking had created the tumours and on a deeper level had triggered the genes for breast cancer inherited from my mother's side of the family. Through depression, I no longer had the will to live and my daily thoughts had reflected this and so my cells had responded accordingly. During the first session she also asked me a very important question:

"*Do you think you can cure your cancer yourself?*"

I thought about it for a moment and then answered:

"Yes."

The moment I answered her, my voice of intuition also replied to me:

"Yes, but you need to find the right shaman."

Here was this word again. I had connected with it in the past in my workshops and my meeting with Kristos and Foster Perry. However, Kristos in his role as the seer took precedence over the shamanic healing as they both agreed this was what I needed most - to introduce some options and clarity to the difficulties facing me at that time. I now felt confused as to who this 'right shaman' was and where I might find this person? Was I already in the right place, or did I need to search somewhere else?

As I continued with my two sessions allocated for Gosia, I realised it was never about 'fighting' cancer, it was about 'de-creating' it, since it was my mind and body together that had created it. Gosia invited me to her workshop at the beginning of 2016 and the theme was about planning the year ahead and getting what you wanted. By meeting other powerful women, it would help to empower me and give me a focus for the year. Before saying goodbye, she asked me if I had had any acupuncture sessions and I replied that she was the second person to suggest this. I don't usually wait for a third time as I felt that the universe was trying to tell me something and so it was back to Sonia to rearrange my last sessions at the Haven. Acupuncture it was to be.

On 12th January 2016, I first met Christopher for one of my four last free sessions which I was now using for acupuncture. I think my name had been entered as a replacement for someone who had changed their appointment and so I was not the client he was expecting to see. He smiled gently and then greeted me with the words:

"I'm glad you recognised me."

I thought these words were a little curious but I didn't dwell on them until afterwards. He offered me the choice of the lift or the stairs, which I was pleased about. It is these small things that become significant when you are losing your strength. For me, the ability to climb stairs was a big thing after my side effects with anastrozole. I had to exert myself to keep pace with the speed he reached the top and all the time I could do things like this, it made me feel better. We entered a beautiful room, the Jade room. Here again light was filtering through another chakra window - wow what a place to have therapy! The first consultation was about talking to me and I found myself blurting out about past abuse and my stressful job that I was hoping to eventually leave as I was so tired. We also discussed my lack of sleep and my fasting and he told me it was now time to nourish myself. I also showed him the Tibetan herbs I was taking and explained about the Essiac tea. He smelt the herbs and said he had come across something similar when in India and they had come from the Himalayas. He asked me if I had seen Gosia and then asked me if I meditated. I mentioned about the use of drifting off to sleep with Premal & Miten on my MP3 player but that on the whole I had not meditated properly for over two years. I removed my shoes and socks after he had checked my tongue and pulses and I got onto the treatment table. He began inserting the acupuncture needles. I had no idea what to expect as I had never experienced them before. I felt tingling in my feet and then one was inserted in my right foot and I felt for a moment a searing pain in one of my top right back molars - the last crowned tooth I had left. I didn't say anything because I knew what this was about. Last year, one by one, my crowned teeth had disintegrated. It was as if the body was trying to reject what was inside the tooth. I had grown up in an era where the NHS provided children with free bottles of syrup from a young age - one was called Delrosa rosehip syrup and the other was a thick concentrated orange juice which tasted delicious because it was so sweet. A whole generation was being set up for tooth decay. It was also not heard of to clean babies' first teeth so this sugary substance clung to the teeth for hours and, to make matters worse, it was frequently given in a baby's bottle or feeding mug. Although we didn't consume many sweets when we were young, every Sunday, when coming back from church, we did collect a quarter of a pound of toffee crunch - the name says it all. So by the time I reached my twenties I had a fair number of fillings which, as they got larger and larger to fill, eventually turned into root canal fillings and crowns. As my body rejected the crowns one by one, I became curious and I looked online. I found some research had been done on breast cancer and root canal fillings. There certainly appeared to be a link; and it was also suggested that keeping a dead tooth, packing it full of chemicals and stripping out the nerves and then finally putting a crown over the top was not the best way forward because the tooth was dead - why keep something dead in your mouth? So when the acupuncture caused the pain to go through my tooth, I was not bothered - clearly there was a connection. The only thing I knew about acupuncture at that time was that it acted on meridians in your body and improved the energy flow and I was familiar with energies from my reiki training. Once the needles were inserted, Christopher sat down at the desk and began to go through some papers. I was finding the noise

Chapter 8 - The Haven

irritating and for some inexplicable reason I wanted to be alone. I no sooner had sent out the thought when he got up and left the room. I lay on the therapy bed with my eyes closed and a deep sense of relaxation came over me. It was not the sort of relaxation where you are going into sleep but the relaxation of meditation, albeit much deeper than I have ever experienced before. I was becoming aware of my body but at tissue level as if I was doing a mental body scan of it. It felt really comfortable and I enjoyed the session. Afterwards, as he went down the stairs ahead of me, he looked at his wrist watch and I suddenly wanted to laugh. It reminded me of the white rabbit in *Alice in Wonderland* when he looks at his large pocket watch and announces that he is late for a very important date. This analogy of *Alice in Wonderland* became more appropriate as time went on. My next session was due in February and in the interim period I continued with my usual regime of herbs, medication and exercise and slowly I started to feel some strength returning.

CHAPTER 9

The Fire Element and The Burrotrek

My second session of acupuncture was scheduled for 9th February 2016. I was again taken to the lovely room with the stained-glass window. My pulses and tongue were checked, and there was a brief chat about how I felt. I was still low and tired at this stage with very little mental and physical energy. I removed my shoes and socks in preparation for the needles, lay down on the table and closed my eyes. I now felt a little more ready for the session than before, when it was unknown. However, this time as the needles were applied to my feet, I could feel the equivalent of small electric currents passing into my feet. It felt like I was being plugged into the mains. As Christopher continued to place the needles into my legs and feet at the various points, I suddenly shot into red light. It was so sudden and I had never seen red light in meditation before. I was so startled I told him I could see bright red light. I remember his quiet reply which also seemed extraordinary at the time: "That's really good because we are working on the fire element." I had no idea what the fire element was in relation to working on my body. I had briefly touched on the elements in my workshops in the past but more in a mystical sense. It reminded me of the stories I had read in childhood of Merlin conjuring up the elements and stars coming off his wand. Once the needles were in place, Christopher left the room and I lost all sense of time, of the room, and of the feel of the treatment table I was on. I was travelling ever deeper into red light. It made my mind feel energised and I tuned into my body. My heart felt strange as if it hurt and was sore and my chest felt tight as if I hadn't breathed deeply in a long time. Christopher had asked me earlier if I had any palpitations

Chapter 9 - The Fire Element and The Burrotrek

and I answered "No". But as I tuned into my body, I was sure I had but chose to ignore them. Christopher came back into the room periodically to place additional needles in my arms and hands and then finally to remove them. I found it difficult to get up and my feet felt so strange - I referred to them as 'Little Mermaid Legs', when the story described the transition from a fish's tail to legs. As I left the Haven, I marvelled at what I had just experienced and I wanted to know more about this fire element. How could you feel so amazing after two sessions of acupuncture?

After the first session and then the meditation in red light, I felt a new strength entering my body. An overpowering desire to live was returning. It had seemed a very long time since I had trekked in Peru and now I wanted to feel the sun on my back again and the earth beneath my feet. My younger son was studying in Barcelona University and I felt that I would like to experience Spain once more. I had not been there since I was in my twenties when I had hitchhiked with my good friend, Annette, from my nurse training days. I thought more and more about where I wanted to go and started to give a voice to it. In my dance class, someone mentioned the book *Spanish Steps* by Tim Moore and how he had trekked the Camino with a donkey. This sounded so beautiful that I went into Waterstones book shop and there, sure enough, was a copy of the book. I sat at home reading and the idea of trekking with a donkey became more and more appealing. I googled 'trekking with donkeys' but all that came up was trekking in France. I was still sure that it had to be Spain and I remembered my son telling me that the Spanish for donkey was burro. I googled 'burro trek' and there was the holiday I was looking for - nine days in all, starting at Sant Climent Sescebes and finishing at the Costa Brava. I could sense the excitement rising but at the same time I was a little worried about whether I should really be doing this. I had had two sessions of acupuncture and felt amazing and as I looked in the mirror, I could see that the colour was returning to my face and the tired haggard look was beginning to fade.

On the weekend before leaving for Spain, my friend Rosemary and I went for supper together at a local restaurant before going on to see a film. As I entered the restaurant and went to the table, my eyes went straight to a beautiful picture on the wall. It was very aptly named 'Dancing Alone' and the artist was Lynne Davies. The picture is so vibrant, with the dancer in a red dress, and the brush strokes make you feel as though you are caught up in the passion of a flamenco dance. In the background are two lovers whom she is totally oblivious to as she is completely absorbed in her own dance. I could not take my eyes off it and I kept thinking back to the bright red light I had experienced in my session. That night I thought more and more about the picture so I phoned the restaurant. I explained we were going away on holiday and asked if they could reserve it for me as it had been priced and was clearly for sale. The restaurant owner told me it had come from the local art gallery and they would reserve it for me until I came back. I could imagine this beautiful picture in just the right environment for it, a place where not only could I recover but, one day, female clients could come and receive counselling.

On 9th March I flew to Barcelona with Rosemary, who had been my trekking partner in Peru. She was the ideal companion as she had grown up with horses and other animals and a donkey would certainly not faze her. Moreover, she still knew nothing about me having cancer and it was something therefore that I didn't need to talk about or even give it a thought for the whole nine days. Arriving in a foreign country without the language took me back to my younger days of hitchhiking without a care in the world and, above all, having fun and meeting new people. The first bit of fun began with trying to withdraw money. Having found the ATM, I could not understand how to put the card into the machine to draw the money but it wasn't long before a young man, anxious to practise his English, came to our aid. Clutching my 300 euros, I then went to the Crystal shop for a Spanish SIM card for my phone. However, as the shop was so busy there was no chance of putting this into the phone and getting it working so we made our way to the shuttle bus from Terminal 1 to 2. Once again, a lovely young person overheard our conversation about needing to buy a ticket for Figueres and, acting like our guardian angel, she told us exactly where we needed to get off to buy it. It was a two-hour train journey to Figueres and during this time I got my SIM card into the phone and, with some help from our Spanish fellow travellers on the train, managed to work out how the regional codes worked. I was then able to make contact with Denise, who would pick us up at Figueres Vilafant railway station. On arrival at the station, we recognised each other instantly - a tall young lady, with a knitted tea cosy hat, an outdoor weathered look and a lovely earthy smell about her.

From the station we drove out to the field to meet the donkeys. Cesar and Mosquit were to be our companions for the journey. I instantly felt I wanted to be with Cesar - a seasoned traveller, 22 years old, the old wise philosopher as Denise described him. Mosquit was 4 and looked like he would need some firm handling; Rosemary was the woman for

Chapter 9 - The Fire Element and The Burrotrek

that and I had no doubt she would soon lick him into shape. After we had met the donkeys, Denise dropped us at our first booked accommodation with Roberto at El Pati de l'Albera. He was a delightful host but unfortunately the nights were still very cold, particularly so close to the mountains, and the room was freezing. We looked at the one blanket on each of our beds and the radiator pumping heat out into the universe through a large gap under the door and decided this did not look promising for a good night's sleep. We went out for supper in the local café and managed to find an English-speaking girl who helped us order an omelette, salad and a glass of wine. I had not been drinking much wine since my diagnosis but this was my holiday and I was going to enjoy every moment of it. The local wine proved to be delicious without the heavy feeling you got from the cheap supermarket plonk back home. On return from our supper, there was no sign of Roberto and we knew we had to survive the night so moving round the guest house bedrooms like Tom Thumb and Hunca Munca out of Beatrix Potter's *Tale of Two Bad Mice* we raided the freshly made beds of each of their blankets and scuttled back to our room. This was not a good introduction to our first night, particularly as we were spending the next night here too and I felt guilty because I had been the one who had booked the holiday and accommodation. However, both Rosemary and I had been brought up by Catholic nuns and this adds a whole new dimension to stoic, so like the Girl Guide motto of 'Be prepared' I think we were ... for just about every occasion in life. We unpacked our bag of clothes and wore just about everything we could find: two sets of trousers, jumpers, waistcoats. It mattered not that we looked like Michelin men – we eventually slept warm.

On day two, after a generous breakfast, off we went to the field again to learn about our new holiday companions. Cesar became mine and Mosquit for Rosemary. I learnt grooming, hoof picking and how to put a cross-shaped carrier on top of my donkey with a blanket underneath for comfort. We then placed our army saddle bag over the top with our luggage. The first day was to be a simple round trip through a small vinery. En route, we found a delightful village called Vilartoli and, since we had forgotten to draw out any money, we had eight euros for lunch between us. A beautiful tapas lunch later, with a lot of interest from the locals, we found when we got back that Roberto had already received pictures and been messaged about us on Facebook. The donkeys had clearly attracted a lot of attention as this was the first time that they had visited this particular village. We wondered at this since we thought that

Denise's groups must be well known. However, this was to be the start of a hilarious inability to use the GPS and we found that we had gone completely off track and had definitely done a round trip but not the one planned. We untacked our friends back at the field and I loved the way the moment Cesar was free of his burden that he would lie in the field with a complete smile on his face, roll onto his back and kick his legs in the air. What a way to finish a day's work! This was one of the many things my four-legged companion was to teach me.

That night Roberto showed us around Peralada and, after a beautiful walk around the grounds of the castle, we went for a superb meal of cod in sauce and goat's cheese salad washed down with red wine. For the holiday, my careful diet was to go out of the window but I had a feeling deep inside that although I needed to watch my cancer diet very closely, the diet was not the major factor for me in this disease. I felt so alive and so excited at the prospect of more days of travel. That night we went back to our same accommodation only this time it was warm as the heater had been on all day and there were ample blankets on the bed.

On day three, we were off to Espolla and would sleep the night at a castle in Can Salas. But we discovered the GPS batteries needed changing before leaving Sant Climent Sescebes. Getting the back off to change the batteries proved to be the ultimate test and as we went from shop to shop it became ever more intriguing that someone appeared to have designed an instrument of such complexity that even how to access the batteries was to remain a mystery. Even the butcher who attacked the back with a large carving knife finished up cutting himself in his effort to prove that this must be simple. As we were about to give up, we recognised a friend of Roberto's from the night before whom Roberto had referred to as a 'donkey whisperer'. It appeared his talents went further and, having located a small ring at the back of the GPS, he simply turned it like a door handle and there were the batteries. With our newly working GPS, we said goodbye to Roberto and with the GPS pointing that we should take a left out of the village and Roberto insisting it was to the right, we were all wrong from the start. But this was to be the way of our holiday throughout and we developed an innate way of finding our way to our destination each night without a clue how we had got there. Poor Denise I think despaired of these rather eccentric English women to whom she had entrusted her donkeys. When she printed off our GPS map at the end of the holiday as a souvenir, I think she could not believe her eyes, particularly as on one occasion we had trekked through army territory. On day three, we should have seen a lake, an old

Chapter 9 - The Fire Element and The Burrotrek

picturesque village and many other noteworthy attractions but since we had set off in the wrong direction from the start the chances of this was remote and became increasingly remote through the day. We trekked more than our 10 kilometres but we stopped along the way, let our donkeys rest, and nibbled our packed lunches - nothing seemed to matter. We eventually found our castle accommodation after lots of sign language and gestures and were met by a lovely elderly gentleman. It was a joy to be in his company and with sign language he told us the story of Catalonia and if they get true independence then the donkey will be at the centre of their flag. In his cellar he made olive oil soap and we also bought bottles of fresh olive oil which he had pressed himself. After a wholesome breakfast we were ready for the road again and lots of locals came to wave us off. Seeing us together with the donkeys seemed to bring joy to their faces.

On day four, we were trekking from Espolla to Rabós and, in spite of being armed with a GPS and a map, managed to go completely wrong. But it was a beautiful hike and by now I was really getting to know Cesar and getting into a stride with him. They myth about donkeys being stubborn is simply not true - they take their time to weigh up a situation and trust only themselves to find the right way for them. While we were thinking about how to get around a particularly difficult fencing area and were preparing to take off the bags to allow the donkeys to get through, Cesar looked on with quiet amusement. Then, just as we had a plan of action he upped and squeezed through the gap with no trouble at all and stood at the other side watching us with a quizzical look on his face, as though he were wondering what we were still doing on the wrong side of the fence. I loved also how, as he walked along, he would fill his mouth with delicious herbs and grass from chosen spots and amble down the road munching until he could fill up again. Although we did not know where we were, we magically arrived at our next guest house where we met Margarita. She had folded up her life in Canada to live in Spain after her father had left the house to her. She was an alternative therapist, herbalist and a Qigong therapist by trade. This was the next piece of puzzle I was being given in a very subtle way. I had heard the word Qigong before from the days when I had learnt tai chi. I had always thought of it as 'a medical form of tai chi' and composed of static poses. Her intention was to open a retreat and teach and use her skills. She had a young French-Canadian girl, Coco, staying with her who did all the cooking and I have never tasted such delicious vegetarian food in my life. Coco was full of life and seemed to get a real pleasure out of preparing the food. When I think about it now, I would say she put 'love' into the food and that is what made it so special. Before we left, Margarita showed us her daughter's room, which was like entering a beautiful cave with a round ceiling and clay walls; it was immensely spiritual and perfect for meditation. Again, another piece was being imparted to me.

After saying goodbye to Margarita and Coco, we were ready for day five, which led us in the sunshine through vineyards to Garriguella. We stopped en route to picnic in the sun while our friends were relieved of their luggage for a while and tethered on a rope to enjoy their lunch. We arrived in plenty of time and enjoyed a beautiful hot tub after a day of trekking. By now we had abandoned all hope of ever using the GPS and I had taken to a map and compass. I was beginning to feel like a million dollars and as I looked in the mirror, I could not believe the ruddy complexion and bright eyes that looked back at me. This was no dying woman!

Day six and we were now out along the Pyrenees and this proved to be the best trek of all. The day was hot and it was our longest day. I didn't have a care in the world, I was miles from nowhere and felt totally self-reliant. Cesar had taught me so much - about survival, self-preservation, joy, freedom, really 'seeing' nature all around me. I appreciated so much that I was able to amble along beside him with clear blue Mediterranean skies above and the warm sun on my skin, gently turning it brown, boosting the vitamin D to aid my recovery. As Cesar was slower than Mosquit I could talk to him out loud, letting go of my fears as I walked and knowing that there was no judgement about what I had chosen to do, no need to justify why I was not doing what everyone else was doing and wanting to scream out "But I am not everyone else - I am me". I was not burdening him in the same way as you would if you had been walking with a friend talking cancer, particularly as my friend's brother was in the last stages of the disease and was awaiting his next dose of chemotherapy. I could not and did not want to weigh her down on such a beautiful holiday. Besides, Cesar had probably heard it or sensed it all before and clearly having reached the ripe old age of 22 he had decided unlike humans not to take any of it on board! Perhaps the most exciting thing of all about being with Cesar was that my sense of smell was returning. I have always had a strong sense of smell. When I lived in India, I could smell the rain several days before the monsoon broke and one of my all-time favourite smells is when rain first hits the ground after a dry hot summer. When I became ill, I noticed that this was no longer as powerful as it used to be. Just before we got to our last lap of the mountains and my friend was beginning to wonder when we would see the sea, I smelt it. I was so excited. We still had a distance to go but I could SMELL the sea.

Chapter 9 - The Fire Element and The Burrotrek

I wanted to shout it from the mountain tops. Each morning, I could smell Cesar as I brushed him. His soft coat smelt of the sweet herbs he had eaten as he would suddenly veer off to the other side of the road and begin grazing on some tasty plant. There was nothing wrong with his sense of smell at his ripe old age. This loss of sense of smell was clearly another symptom of my ill health but if you told your GP they would want you to eventually get your nose examined, whereas the fact of the matter is your senses are slowly shutting down because you are dying. Later I researched this phenomenon of smell and found that Dr Jayant Pinto, an Associate Professor of Surgery at the University of Chicago, described it so well, stating:

"We think loss of smell is like the canary in the coalmine. It doesn't directly cause death, but it's a harbinger - an early warning that something has gone badly wrong, that damage has been done."

We began our descent to the Costa Brava and stayed at the Hostal Totsompops, in Colera, which had every conceivable picture, effigy and ornament of an octopus you could imagine. It was pleasant enough but arriving back into civilisation was not really what we wanted. The good, fresh, mountain village food now gave way to plastic cheese and supermarket bread- we knew we had left real Spain behind. We spent the next day trekking around the area and then back for to say goodbye to our friends as Denise came to collect them. That night Rosemary received the news that her brother had passed away. Although it was a sad occasion for her, it was also a blessing as his next round of chemo would have been an experimental one and she knew that neither of them wanted to witness the effects. Another beautiful thing was that because Rosemary was away on holiday, he took the opportunity to visit the person he had loved all his life and she was with him when he died. If Rosemary had not been on holiday, he may have made a different decision to stay close to his family instead. And so, our holiday came to an end and only the memories remain but for me it was a real turning point in my recovery.

During the trek I had sent an email to the staff at the Haven - sending them pictures and thanking them for their amazing support and help. At this stage, the length of life I had left did not matter as much as the quality. I was having the time of my life out in the open air, trekking through vineyards with a donkey - what more could you ask from life. I had not had so much fun in years. There were times during the day that I marvelled at how well I felt considering I had two tumours supposedly taking away my life force and how two sessions of acupuncture could make me feel like this and I still had two more free sessions to go.

ॐ
CHAPTER 10

White Light, the Cosmos and Infinity

It was now nearing the end of March and I was ready for my third session. The high feeling I had had throughout my holiday remained with me so that when I got to the Haven, I felt a bit of a charlatan. I found it difficult to handle the question of how far I had got with my treatment when I sat next to another visitor in the waiting area. People came in either with their head bald or an assortment of different scarves and I was sitting there feeling fantastic. I had once or twice ventured that I was not doing conventional treatment as I had on the introductory day but then I could see in their eyes a look of astonishment and pity as though I was digging my own grave. So I learnt to sit quietly and read. At their little library, I was immediately drawn to a book called *Quantum Healing* by Deepak Chopra. It took me back to when my son was studying quantum physics at university. He had had no love for the subject as it didn't seem to follow any logic. The more I read of the book, the more sense it was making and particularly the idea of going back to the root cause and the tumour at cellular level. I decided this was something I needed to know more about. How I wished I had just a small smattering of knowledge of this type of physics and I vowed that if I survived it would be a topic that I would get at least a basic knowledge of. I began thinking about the concept of taking your body back in time to when the tumour first began - that division of the cells when they first deviated from the original blueprint - and identifying what was happening in the body at that time for it to happen. With these thoughts in my head, Christopher appeared and he thanked me for my email and how much all the staff had enjoyed it - I had become known as 'the donkey lady'.

Chapter 10 - White Light, the Cosmos and Infinity

He noted the book I had been reading and he stopped to chat to a colleague. He ended the conversation by jokingly saying we were off to do some quantum healing!

We entered the beautiful room of light and he remarked how well I looked and I expressed how well I felt. I mentioned how rewarding his job must be if he got results like this and he replied that he couldn't get results like this with everyone, only with people like me. I was learning by now not to ask too many questions. Christopher with all his Eastern training had clearly taken on board the way of the ancient oriental masters who make the recipient think about the answer for themselves so there is no possibility of misinterpretation since you are the one left doing the interpreting. Sometimes this appeared to take the form of riddles that might take many months to solve. It is rather like being given a bowl of rice to eat using chopsticks for the first time; at first you struggle to even put a few grains into your mouth until slowly you master the technique. Christopher's way of speaking to me in riddles was not dissimilar to the way that the characters spoke to Alice hence, my analogy to *Alice in Wonderland* being intuitively correct at the end of my first session of acupuncture. I instinctively knew I was meant to take the information away and think about it and only if I needed clarity should I ask the question 'Why?' As he inserted the needles, I found myself talking about the trek and also about the picture I had bought and I described it. He asked me about the colour of the dancer's dress and at this stage I had already closed my eyes. I could see the bright red flame colour, but as the needles were inserted, I shot into white light. It was so sudden and the vibration was so high. It was like the sun when it is so bright in the sky that you cannot look at it with the naked eye. I had never seen white light before. When I have done deep meditation in the past, I have had various shades of purple from pale lilac to deep, deep purple like that of a royal velvet robe. I was so astonished, that I told Christopher I was now in white light. I remember the door closing behind him and then I travelled up and up ever further into white light and then mind and body lay still. I was in a void of intense white light and completely at peace. I lost all touch with time, place and space but I recall at one point when I was gradually entering more into the sensation of my body that I could see the cancer cells on the left side of my body. They were grey towards the periphery but much darker where the tumour was more solid. I could also sense a depletion of energy on this side of the body as if there was a really sluggish flow like a river that had been dammed.

All too soon the session was over and as the needles were taken out, I expressed what a beautiful session of light it had been; Christopher told me that that was cosmic orbit. I had begun to research the five elements already and now here was a new word for me to find out about. One day these words would become completely familiar when I had learnt the language of energy from the Chinese perspective.

My fourth session on 26th April was to lead me to a profound new depth of understanding. Before my acupuncture appointment, I attended the London clinic for an ultrasound scan. There was a bit of a mix-up from the GP surgery and they had sent on my mammogram details but not the last ultrasound scan that I had had done with the NHS. They thought I had requested another mammogram but I was very definite that I did not want one of these, only a scan. Mammograms are controversial in that there are conflicting opinions about squashing the breast with its tumour or tumours between metal plates and then irradiating it. Biopsies are the same, by piercing into the tumour there is the risk of spreading the cancer cells. Although my tumour was originally picked up by mammogram, better education and taking care of my body would have picked this up without having had to do these diagnostics. Similarly, before the regular mammograms, GPs were trained to palpate and our family doctor when I was a child was extremely skilled at this. He found my mother's breast lump and he diagnosed my sister with acute appendicitis at the age of two and saved her life. Another GP had insisted that she had gastritis but had clearly not done the vital pressing on the right iliac fossa area of the abdomen which would have responded with guarding pain to give the clue to the real problem. In hindsight I would certainly have left out the biopsy and would not have had the second mammogram after they had found the lumps on the first one. Ultimately, the ultrasound gave them more information and given my family history and two tumours, it was obvious that it was malignant. On this occasion since they had no previous scan images to compare, they admitted that it was more difficult as everyone's technique and angle of measurement is slightly different. The long and the short of it was that they measured both lumps as being slightly larger. I wasn't really too worried as when you are measuring something in such small measurements it is more difficult to be accurate.

Later, as Christopher inserted the acupuncture needles, we had a brief chat. I mentioned the scan and told him that after the last session I had received intuitively and very clearly that I should be doing Qigong to complement his therapy. This had been further reinforced for the second time by my meeting with Margarita in Spain. Although I had done several

Chapter 10 - White Light, the Cosmos and Infinity

different forms of tai chi in the past and been shown a few Qigong exercises at the end of some of these sessions, I knew very little about it. I had always considered it a form of exercise used for the elderly to assist them with balance and general well-being. I had no idea where these classes would materialise from but nothing seemed impossible these days. It was then as we chatted that I finally learnt that the silver zizzy things I had seen at the sea when I was a child were called chi. I remember feeling a little overwhelmed that, after all these years, someone could confirm their existence and that I was in fact not mad at all but could see things that not everyone could see. It's rather like saying a dog is colour blind - although they may not have the cones in their retinal system like humans and therefore we assume that colour vision is not there, we still do not know exactly what they see. They may have a depth of vision that we are totally unaware of at this time, and their sense of smell more than makes up for what they may be lacking in sight.

Christopher left the room and I very quickly entered a deep state but this time it was more profound than I had ever experienced in any meditation, including my white light experience. It was also different from my OBEs when I was a child. Just as in my previous sessions, I lost the concept of time and place and began to travel. I travelled for a while in a tunnel of light similar to that described in books that I had read many years ago when studying near-death experiences (NDEs). I did not feel as though I was going to be getting out at the end of the tunnel - the bright intense light was a long way ahead. Somewhere along the tunnel it felt as though I veered off at a different place and began travelling rapidly. The next thing I knew I was travelling through the cosmos into the most beautiful, radiant colours of bright, bright light, blues and reds and purples and black and white light that is not there on the earth plane in such intensity. There also appeared to be objects like rocks moving through space rather like seeing the pictures from the Hubble telescope except my mind was actually travelling through them. I carried on travelling until finally I reached a somewhat grey still area of 'nothingness'. I do not know what else to call it, nor do I really have the words to describe it. It is like being in a vast expanse of fog but not as dense, where you can see nothing around you at all. It just seemed to go on forever. I remember clearly asking in my head:

"*Is this all that there is?*"

Again, I continued to travel and I asked:

"*Is there more?*"

And again, I sped on and on. Several more times I asked:

"*And is there more?*"

Each time I found myself travelling at a fast speed ever deeper through the same nothingness but strangely I felt that in this nothingness was everything. Finally, when I asked again, I now had a sense of knowing and then I was being told:

"*There is no beginning and there is no end.*"

Was this then the concept of infinity? It just is - no beginning and no end? And then I was asked:

"*What do you need - what more do you want? You have now seen everything.*"

I replied in my head:

"*Nothing.*"

I was then asked:

"*What do you need to go back for? Do you want to go back?*"

I replied:

"*No.*"

I was asked again:

"*Do you need to go back?*"

Immediately I thought of my dog, all alone with no one to care for her when she had cared so well for me. It wasn't that I didn't love my children but they could manage without me since they were now grown. Physically I wouldn't need to push myself through work anymore. I didn't need to do the things I had been doing for a living to help everyone else exist that made me feel so tired and weak, physically and mentally. The struggle now seemed impossible to continue with. Over the years I had become like a well that was slowly being emptied with no rain to top it up. Everyone would be ok. I had to leave sometime and was there anything more to really do? My dog was the only being who really needed me as my two sons were living away from home and my husband at this stage had no idea or interest in looking after her. It was not until sometime later when she too nearly died that he was to become involved in her care as he realised how much she mattered to the family and he loved her in his own way. But for the moment, having seen infinity and the profound stillness and peace of it all, why would I choose to come back to everything on the earth plane? So what I was really being asked was:

"*Do you want to live or die? The choice is ultimately yours.*"

I knew that this was not going to be the time right now, I was just being shown an option on this particular journey and if I wished to, I could let go very easily in the not too distant future. I found myself giving the reply:

"*I need to go back for my dog.*"

Chapter 10 - White Light, the Cosmos and Infinity

I found myself thinking that she did not choose the life she was given with me and she had no one else to care for her. Humans at least have choices as they grow older. I had a rather curious thought then that animals and plants do not choose what happens to them – but do we?

Next, I found I was speeding back through where I had come from at such a rapid speed that I could not comprehend even the outline of the tunnel. Back, back to the earth plane and as I entered the earth's atmosphere, I could see how dark it all was. It was how you might imagine trying to land a plane at Heathrow Airport on a dark foggy night with no lights. It was not like the stillness I had left behind, which felt that all creation was possible. Here I could feel the heaviness of war and pollution and dirt and disease. As I hovered between this realm and the earth, I again had a clear picture of my cancer cells but this time they were moving around almost like amoebae. They appeared to be changing shape and it was then that I had the feeling that what Deepak Chopra had described in his book was indeed possible but I did not know how. I was aware that Christopher had returned to the room, was taking my pulse and began taking out the needles. I did not try or need to explain anything because I felt that he knew. This made me more intrigued – were we during treatment sessions sharing the same consciousness? Do we all share the same consciousness? Do we have different wavelengths we tune in at? Was this what telepathy of old was among tribal people when they knew if a member of their tribe was in trouble and needed help and then they knew exactly where they were and what was wrong? The session left me with so many questions but also a deep sense of peace. If, as I had been shown, there is no beginning and there is no end, and we are all part of the same consciousness, why would you need to fear death? And if we were all part of the same consciousness and expanded it for the greater good, what would this be like to live in?

As I was preparing to leave, I explained what I had seen with the cancer cells and said that I thought we could 'dissolve' them. He didn't make any reply and we settled on a date for my next appointment.

When I left the Haven, it was late afternoon. I stopped near the station at Fulham Broadway to get a coffee as I felt a bit of grounding was needed to go back on the Tube and even more so to go back home. All the way home I could not stop thinking about what had happened – it was all so incredible. And why, above all, was this happening to me? That night I went to the kitchen to do my wifely duties of cooking and clearing dishes and when I was asked how my day was, I replied with the usual:

"*Fine. How was yours?*"

Cancer – A Magical Quest

How could you begin to explain what had happened during the course of the day? I did not want to risk the same ridicule I had experienced as a child and normalising was something I had become very good at over the years. Once supper was cooked, I remember feeling exhausted and as soon as my head hit the pillow I fell into a completely deep, dreamless sleep.

The next day I bought the book *Quantum Healing* and I decided to print off a colourful picture of DNA from the internet and do some visualisation techniques with it including elves with vacuum cleaners sucking up the cancer cells to fairies with wands doing a Harry Potter job on them! In my inner world I created sparkles on the DNA and imagined the healthy cells talking to the cancerous cells. A few years earlier, in meditation at the Spiritualist Church, I had seen how trees and plants communicate with each other. The notion of 'fairy lights' is not so far-fetched. I saw tiny little blue/white lights like those used for Christmas tree decorations, flashing on and off as they 'communicate'. During storms, the lights that I had seen in meditation dim and barely flash and this communicates to the birds and animals so that they quickly seek shelter. I suspect that animals also have the same sense of communication with each other and their world around them, we are just not aware of it yet.

Shortly after the fourth session of acupuncture, I was again guided by my intuitive voice back to Waterstones and there on their notice board was an advert for Dragon and Tiger Qigong classes with Simon. The hours suited perfectly and it was not long before I joined the class. As I began doing the exercises, I knew that I would train more fully in this discipline but I also wanted to find out more about the five elements described in Chinese medicine and the same discipline that Christopher had trained in, in his study of acupuncture. Shortly after my session I sourced a school of Elemental Qigong in London and without any hesitation applied for the training. As I did so, I thought back to the words of my seer, Kristos, who said that I would work in energy work and shamanism. Did this mean that life was predestined? How else could he have seen this? After all, when he had delivered this message I did not go out and actively seek this path. Was it perhaps because he had mentioned this to me that it allowed my mind to expand and attract the information and people to me? Here I was, less than a year after meeting Foster and Kristos, and all these events were happening in my life as if by magic. I would no sooner think something than it would appear without any effort on my behalf.

CHAPTER 11

The Primordial Child

Intuitively, I had known that I had to go back in time to find the root cause of this disease. Emotionally and psychologically, I had unpicked all the events that had led up to it. I had begun to feng shui my home as Christopher had suggested in my last session prior to the acupuncture. His sessions were always so full of wisdom as he lit the way through the minefield of what was so much more than just the tumour. I knew that a cluttered home meant a cluttered mind and even if I could not clear everyone else's clutter I could at least do my own. I came across so many papers that filled me with the pain, grief, sadness, shame, anger, turmoil and guilt of those years. From old letters to the children's school, to the tribunal file of the medical centre, to visa statements showing how hard the financial struggle had been. It was all SO SAD. Why was I holding on to it all? It wasn't because I wanted to, it was because I had just never allowed myself the time to deal with it all until now. I thought about when my father had moved house after the death of my mother. She had been so orderly with very few possessions and left everything organised so that, apart from her clothes, there was no need for a house clearance. Like her life, in death too, you had no sense of who she was, just a shell of what she could have been. On the other hand, my father was a hoarder and kept a garage full of bits and pieces that might be useful and, to be fair, he was gifted at DIY and recycling but it presented a marathon job to clear it all. He had also been so busy working that he never had time to sort his life out and then it just became a comfortable clutter to have around him. I was determined I didn't want all these sad old memories left for someone else to clear away. I wanted to leave a worthwhile legacy that could be used by those who were meant to receive it. What good would it do to hold onto this sort of past? The past was over and it was time to start afresh without regrets. If I was choosing to live then it was time to do just that. I had learnt from it all, or so I thought, but I didn't need to carry it like a heavy load. I prepared everything ready for the shredding machine. As I cleared it, the more I found in cupboards and drawers and there was still the garage to go.

In the garage I began to find myself. Under the pile of dust, cobwebs and rodent droppings emerged my spinning wheel, weaving equipment, knitting patterns, some of which I had designed myself, and balls of wool with unfinished knitting projects. As I worked my way through the mess, I started to see what the cause of my disease was really all about – there in cases and old trunks were what had made my heart sing from a young age. My books on past life regression. There was *More Lives than One* by Jeffrey Iverson – my younger son had obtained a copy for one of my birthdays and written inside the cover of it to remind me how special I was. There were all my old hypnotherapy notes from the National College of Hypnotherapy and Psychotherapy where I had studied back in 1991. I later used this precious knowledge to help a family member release their childhood trauma. I had read Joe Keeton's book *The Power of the Mind*, describing healing through hypnosis and regression. *Beyond the Light* by P.M.H. Atwater was underneath the pile, where I got my first illumination about near-death experiences. And there were books on the life of Carl Jung; sand tray therapy; ancient civilisations and their cultures and beliefs; illustrations of cave paintings around the world; oracle cards and ruins; astrology; and my reiki certificates. I went on lifting these beautiful gems out, one by one as if on an archaeological dig. The garage became transformed into Aladdin's cave as I rediscovered all these treasures.

In my teens and early twenties, while most of my friends were into fashion, make-up, latest hair styles and boyfriends, this is where my passion lay. I wanted to know everything there was to know about these subjects and it was so hard to find such books in those days. These were not subjects that were generally talked about in the seventies, let alone studied. They were classified as weird. It was only with a kindred spirit, Brenda, that I could talk, read and share minds late into the night as we feasted on this banquet of knowledge. Even though most of these books were now yellow with age I couldn't wait to take them to safety and rediscover their contents once again. They are the type of books where each time you read, no matter how many times, new information always comes to light. As the depth of your knowledge increases over time, you become more and more open to higher thought processes and greater understanding. Sometimes I realise that I don't even remember whole parts of some books simply because the depth of understanding was not there at the time. Just recently I again came across Lynne McTaggart's book *The Field*. It talks of a life force – the Zero Point Field – connecting the entire universe. I found it a fascinating book when I first read it and remembered the name of Fritz-Albert Popp and had made some jottings in a notepad at the time. However, as I reread it now it takes on a whole new meaning. It provides scientific explanations of how acupuncture and homeopathy work and descriptions of how Popp saw that the light in cancer patients' cells was going out because they had lost their natural periodic rhythm. Just as Christopher had ignited the fire element in my body several months earlier, effectively bringing it back to life, so my mind was now reciprocating and dancing its fire dance with excitement. Others had gathered all these amazing concepts over time, leading this civilisation into rediscovering what the ancient civilisations had known for years. This disease for me was not just about an inherited gene pool or the stresses of life. It was something much more profound. It is the word that is omitted from conventional therapies and medical training. It is SPIRIT – the life force that unites us all, the driving will to live and express ourselves. I realised that I had not done this – really lived or expressed myself – for years. Who I was had been buried under the burden of daily living, paying bills, cooking meals, washing and ironing clothes, looking after others and running like Roger Bannister for his four-minute mile. I was on that treadmill of life not daring to stop to ask why I was doing it and where I was going. As I sat and looked around the garage, I thought back to an interview with G. Edward Griffin, the American author of the book *World without Cancer*, in the documentary series *The Truth about Cancer: A Global Quest* by Ty Bollinger. In the interview, Griffin said:

"The present orthodox view is that cancer is a lump or a bump. That's the cancer. That's the assumption. Now if that is true then to get rid of cancer all you have to do is get rid of the lump or the bump and hence we have surgery. Well, that gets rid of the lump or the bump. Or we have chemotherapy, which poisons the lump or the bump if we got rid of it. Or we have radiation, which burns it and got rid of it.

"And you undergo these three therapies and to get rid of the lump or the bump the doctor will say, 'it looks like we got it all'. That famous line, 'We got it all.'

But did they? No, the statistics show that in most cases it comes back. They didn't get it all because that was never the cancer in the first place.

"If you're a farmer and see all these little black spots on your corn leaves and you think, well those are black spots. That's the disease and you get scissors out and you cut all the black spots away. Well, you say, we got it all, right? No, you didn't because that wasn't the disease. What caused those black spots is still present."

Griffin saw the disease as one of deficiency. I thought about this in more depth. Supposing the human is weakened either by stresses in the environment or the mind telling it that it has no will to live. Then the person's nutrition starts to lack vital ingredients such as vitamins for example B17, antioxidants, minerals and trace elements, as Griffin has suggested, so that the human becomes weaker and then the body environment increases in toxicity when we pour sugar into it as a coping mechanism for lack of love. The oxygen levels then get depleted from lack of exercise or shallow breathing resulting from tiredness, anxiety or fear about the environmental factors. Eventually, everything weakens further until disease sets in - 'the black spots on the corn leaves'. It may well be as Popp describes, the light then goes out of the cells. Apart from a natural decline due to aging, what else might cause the decline in light other than environmental factors and ultimately the loss of the will to live? So many women with breast cancer that I have spoken to over the course of time knew exactly what I meant when I asked them the question:

"When did you decide that you no longer wanted to live?"

With this new level of insight, I was now preparing myself for my fifth acupuncture session. The alignment of the numbers was in itself uncanny. I was attending for my 5th session on the 5th day of the 5th month and we were working with the 5 elements - Fire, Earth, Metal, Water and Wood.

I had no expectations as I entered the Haven for my afternoon appointment. After Christopher had greeted me, we made our way to a new room as my free sessions had now finished. It was up on the top floor and the room was very quiet and dark, almost womb like. We chatted for a short while as he inserted the needles and, like all good practitioners, he was aware of my belief systems and my particular affinity at this time to the Medicine Buddha. The Medicine Buddha is said to be blue because it is linked to one of the master healing stones, lapis lazuli. The deep indigo blue is also associated with the third eye area in the centre of the forehead between the eyes and depicts clarity,

Chapter 11 - The Primordial Child

vision and seeing beyond illusion. According to the Buddhist teachings, when we are truly able to recognise sickness and disease as merely a reflection of the lack of light radiating from our own mind, then it no longer has any substantial existence and our suffering disappears. I knew that for me, I was responsible for my own healing and no medicinal potion or surgical procedure could bring about a magical cure. While talking to me, Christopher gave me a very clear and appropriate message – that I must become my own Medicine Buddha and to focus on 'changes' rather than 'healing'. In the exploration of my disease, the wisdom of his words became more apparent. Unless I made changes to my life, everything would remain the same, including the disease that had been caused by my inability to make the appropriate mental and physical changes that were required to live a fulfilled life.

As I lay on the table, alone in the room, I had a sense of an altar where there was a statue of Buddha against the backdrop of the Himalayas. Also on the altar sat a vase of dried lavender and a sacred book with the symbol ॐ on the outside of its ancient cover. I had the impression of being in a very lovely temple deep down underground in a cavern. As I entered deeper into meditation, I entered the void and rested quietly in nothingness, no sound and no visuals. Slowly, in the nothingness, I could see a foetus emerging. It was around 6 months' gestation and beautifully formed with its fingers and toes. Through its translucent body I could see the blood vessels and all the organs in place. It was surrounded by a foetal sac and the umbilical cord floated freely in the void outside. There it lay, quietly resting, as if waiting for the time of its birth. My mind then was taken to my left breast where the tumours were growing and I watched as they were lifted completely out of my breast. I felt such a sense of relief and lightness in that part of my body as if I was a young teenage girl again. I lay at peace, resting and watching the embryo, which was still very much part of my visual experience. My conscious mind tried to understand what I was being shown. I believed it was still part of taking the tumour back to its original DNA and meant that I needed to go on working on clearing my external and internal surroundings. When the session came to an end, I felt so radiant and carefree but overwhelmed with what I was experiencing. Each session was so vastly different and yet taking me ever deeper on my quest. The more I experienced, the more inadequate my knowledge seemed – my understanding of the primordial child was no exception. It was to be almost two years later when the embryo appeared again in meditation and a fellow Qigong student, trained in craniosacral therapy, would explain this to me in much greater depth. It would mean going back even further than the concept of the DNA, back to the Zero Point Field described by Lynne McTaggart in her book *The Field*.

As the weeks passed, I felt elated. I could no longer feel the main tumour and the smaller one had never been palpable. My favourite time of year was approaching and I was looking forward to feeling the sun beating on my back again and being out in the open air, growing organic vegetables and watching everything around me bursting into life. I walked a lot with Iona and my body and mind felt unbelievably healthy. I was meditating on a daily basis using the Premal and Miten's version of the Sanskrit mantra to Vishnu, 'Om Namo Narayanaya', as I had done ever since my diagnosis. Interestingly, I had had no idea in the early days that it was a mantra to Vishnu. Perhaps this was the reason for my powerful vision in the Buddhist Centre. My daily meditations were pure and in white or golden light. I had a sense that even if I died now at this very time, my life had known a bliss that many people don't ever experience in an entire lifetime. I remember waking early one morning and, for the first time in my life, I said to myself:

"*I love and respect you.*"

I continued with my Qigong exercises daily and was excited about starting the five elements training. I did not doubt for a moment that this bliss would now go on forever. If only that were the case! The conditioning of a person is deeply ingrained and it was not long before the old patterns re-emerged and the struggle began again. The higher you reach, the further there is to fall and my freefall was rapid and destructive. Two events made me realise that I had not yet processed the emotions or patterns of behaviour that had led up to the cancer. My younger son came back for a while to live in the family home and my younger sister came from Canada with her children. All of these people around me had major issues in their lives and it was not long before I was feeling tired physically and then weak in both legs. I was having what I called my 'Little Mermaid legs' where they felt like jelly and my chest felt strange and tight. I again started to eat an unhealthy diet consoling myself with biscuits and chocolate as there did not seem the time anymore to just care for myself. My sleep patterns were disrupted because I was choosing to let others' expectations of me once again take over. When I intuited into what was going on, I got back very clearly that it was all about my lungs. As I stifled my creativity as I had done all my life, I felt I could no longer breathe again. I also felt angry with myself because I had come so far and I did not want to slide back into those old ways.

Chapter 11 - The Primordial Child

Yet, I was allowing myself to become stuck in old patterns of behaviour which were familiar and that, to use a cliché, 'moving forward' was becoming increasingly difficult because I was stuck in the past. The main reason that moving forward was difficult was because previously I had allowed myself to free up time to write and, now that I had stopped, I was hearing the old familiar parental words of 'wasting time' and 'what was ever going to become of it'. In a word, I was SCARED – scared that soon I would have no money and I would have to return to the treadmill of work in November and all this beautiful journey would have been for nothing and eventually have no meaning. Interestingly, when I look at this word, it contains another word, SCAR, which has its own significance. These scars of negativity from the past was something that I was going to have to transform sooner rather than later if I was to find a new fulfilled life. It was time to find a way to release this addictive, destructive behaviour lodged in the very cells of my body. I knew once I could do this I would be finally fully well again. I was getting the most beautiful meditations at 3 a.m. just as the world was waking up, but by mid-morning I felt exhausted with absorbing like a sponge all the situations around me. Once again, I could feel the tumour and at times the whole area ached as if to remind me of what I was doing to myself. I was 'listening' but not doing anything about what I was hearing. I had believed that everything would happen easily after my meditation experience in my 5th acupuncture session and the word 'belief' has very strong almost religious connotations of things being set in stone. If I was to carry on bringing changes with my mind and body then change did not fit with the concept of things being set in stone. Change meant a constant flow of movement, adjusting, amending and growing.

    I did not return for my next acupuncture appointment until 14th July 2016. By this time, the energies around me had become really unsettling as my nephew was going through a particularly difficult teenage period. I remember similar times with my sons and although generally it is only a phase, it is for the most part a painful and hurtful one for a mother if you have been carrying the burden of caring for your children single handed. Trying to maintain a sense of peace and stillness with family demands of day trips became difficult. I felt as though I was beginning to lose any sense of serenity that I had carried with me from the Haven for several weeks. One day we were sitting in Hyde Park eating a picnic lunch in between a hop-on hop-off bus trip. It was the hottest day of the summer and my nephew had had another session of disrespect with his mother. As we sat eating, to distract the situation, she asked everyone a hypothetical question:

"If you only had twenty-four hours to live, what would you do?"

My husband said he would take to task everyone who had ever caused him grief while he was alive. My nephew said he would like to be in the army and learn about guns and shooting. I began to drift off and to think about what this would be like for me. I decided I would say goodbye to the family and my dog and make sure I had found her someone to love and look after her. I would then fly to Tibet and find a beautiful mountain to sit by and look out over the scenery below. I would contemplate my life and be grateful for it and then gradually prepare to leave in this frame of mind. Fortunately, I did not get asked what I would do because wars and settling old scores seemed to be the main topic of conversation. So much for distraction. It was at this point I knew I needed something to take me to higher places and texted for an urgent appointment the next day. I was finding the heaviness around me just too difficult a load to carry and, above all, I was losing my connection with the light that I had managed to maintain for so many weeks. This was mainly because I was no longer getting the time or special space to meditate that was vital for my mind and body. I also had not allowed this to happen. This journey, I soon found out, was to require utter dedication and was certainly not for the faint hearted.

ॐ

CHAPTER 12

Detachment

My mind had been unsettled all day as I made my way to the Haven. I had tried to settle myself on the train by reflecting on the London trip a few days earlier with my sister. I wanted to refocus on how it felt to be serene and happy at the roof of the world but I failed to capture that tranquillity. Instead I felt nervous and jumpy and it didn't take long before I attracted a situation in my outer world that reflected my inner one. As I entered the Haven, there was no soothing environment waiting here either. It was a fund-raising day and in full swing even in the afternoon. The normal restful waiting area was full of important visitors, milling around and chatting loudly over cups of tea and coffee. I found an area to sit and immediately disappeared behind my book. The scene in front of me only added to my feelings of disconcertion. Fortunately, Christopher arrived to my rescue and seemed completely unfazed to the point that he didn't even mention all these people gathered on the ground floor. Up we went to the top floor but not to same room as for the fifth session. It had a skylight window and, as it was a warm day, it was open and I could hear the noise from the street. I found that I did not need to say much about the issues that were troubling me. They were already understood as was my frustration with myself. I settled myself on the treatment table, and once Christopher had left, I tried to put my mind into a good place where once again I could transport myself to higher realms. I became aware of a figurine of a black goddess and a picture behind her of the high peaks of the Himalayas. It put me in mind of Black Tara. Tara in Eastern culture represents the Divine Mother and her name means 'Star'. In Tibet she is seen in many forms – a goddess of mysticism and aesthetics, creator and protector of all humans. She is also represented in many colours - Green, White, Red, Yellow, Blue and Black. Black Tara is symbolic of power. I thought about when my sister had sat in the park in London asking us what we would do if we were given 24 hours to live and I had visualised myself sitting alone in the mountains of Tibet. I felt myself saying inwardly that I wanted to assume my own power and go even higher than I had ever been before in my meditations.

However, this was not going to be the day. This was a day that was going to test me beyond even my journey of fear and aloneness back in the early days of my diagnosis. As I lay there trying to settle, I heard two voices coming from outside and heard the words:

"*She has trouble in detaching.*"

I became confused and angry. Was it me that was being discussed? Detaching from what, I thought? What am I supposed to be detaching from? I was now becoming aware of a smell coming from the streets. It smelt of blocked drains and by now I was wondering why I was smelling this awful smell. I was beginning to feel paranoid as I did when I was a child when my mother would undermine my confidence by talking about me as if I was not in the room. I wondered if all this outside stuff was, in some way, of my making. Was it really the street smells or was it something to do with my anger, pain and frustration that I had felt throughout my life, mostly towards myself? This inability to love myself had caused stagnation in my emotions and physical well-being and maybe the outside world was reflecting it back at me. I felt so confused and mixed up. I had come for peace and tranquillity but it was being met with disappointment. Christopher came back into the room to place some more needles and eventually I closed my eyes again and tried to settle. I entered the void but now there were no visuals at all, not even a guiding light. It was just grey and uninviting. I asked inwardly what this was about and heard the reply:

"*You need to detach.*"

I thought about this and again wondered, what did detach mean? If you detach from something or a situation, it meant you were removing yourself from it, cutting yourself off from it. But how did you do this? How could you live detached from everything? Did this mean you had to live without emotions and, if you did, how could you relate to others? Did it mean not to return to the Centre for anymore treatment? I had no answers.

Chapter 12 - Detachment

My session came to an end and I felt disappointed and angry. I had been shown this magical journey up until now but for what purpose if it was to end like this? I might just as well have detached from life right back at the beginning. I did not make a further appointment and as I went on my way home, I was struggling to hold back the tears.

For the next few days, I did not meditate and I could not exert myself to do any Qigong exercises as my body felt uncomfortable and painful at times when I tried. I was feeling deep chest pain and yet I could feel my pulse was getting stronger. I was aware of a tightness in my upper back around the left lung area and I remembered the horrible smell of the last session. I asked myself the same question. Was this part of all the stored anger, hate, pain and frustration that I had felt throughout a lot of my life, mostly towards myself? I had spent a good part of my life thinking I was no good and by this inability to love myself I had created a stagnant pond in my body with no inlet or outflow for my heart. At night when I closed my eyes and tried to contact my guides, there was nothing. No guiding voices, not even my intuitive one. I felt abandoned, as I had as a child. I could not trust anyone, not even myself. Maybe my guides and everything I had experienced throughout life was just make-believe, a coping mechanism to get me through a difficult time and now I didn't even have this to believe in anymore. I began to challenge all of my belief systems. What exactly were these concepts of 'right' and 'wrong', 'good' and 'bad'? Who gave us these concepts? From the moment we are born, depending on the society we grow up in and the religious beliefs we are given, we are conditioned. So if everything I ever believed about everything, including myself, was all conditioned then **Who Was I?** There were no answers coming back. I felt I was just channelling pure consciousness before anyone had put anything into it. NO LIMITING THOUGHTS ABOUT ABSOLUTELY ANYTHING. It reminded me of the type of sensation an astronaut might experience once he got over the terrifying experience that he was no longer tethered to anything, while walking in space. No connections with the NASA control system, no one to talk to or be with, all alone with only himself. I was listening now to only my own voice. It was like attending a philosophy class on my own. I then thought that if you had no concepts about anything and you could just be, then you would be fearless about life and death. If you lived each day as if it was the only day you were experiencing then it would not be about packing every experience that you think you might have missed into the last moments of your life but about being ready to leave at any time with no regrets, no wishes, no needs and with a sense of joy and completion of that moment in time.

I continued to go on pondering this for days on end. As I stood at the kitchen sink preparing food I would look out into the garden and think about who I really was. What was the purpose of all of this life which without conditioning now felt meaningless? The concept of *me* was from my parents, teachers, relatives and friends around me. As I increased these concepts, they were from books and new environments of different cultures and beliefs but these were not me either, they were just a series of information that I had access to. As I walked with my dog and looked at nature around me, I became more awe-struck by how amazing it all was, the sky, the trees, the birds, the small bushes and plants, the insects - each having a remarkable connection and I was the observer. In some ways I envied the trees and the animals that just seemed to get on with life and didn't spend time deliberating over who they were. They just lived. I had no answer as to who I was in all of this and I felt dreadfully alone and lost. There were times when I felt gripped by fear and frozen in time.

When I say I was alone, this was not strictly speaking true. During this time and now, I am fortunate and blessed to have an amazing friend, Agnieszka, who attends Zumba classes with me. She is like an angel, both in looks and inner beauty, with a highly evolved mind and spirit to match. She listened so patiently to my dilemma, over our usual after-class Sunday coffee, and she suggested I read *Ramtha: The White Book*. Ramtha is an enlightened ascended Master Teacher who learnt in his lifetime about the potential of the mind to create and shape our own reality when we do not apply any limiting factors to it. The author, J.Z. Knight, became a channel for Ramtha in order to bring the teachings into book form. When I got home, I ordered it online as Agnieszka felt sure this would help me to understand this new stage of development I was entering into - channelling consciousness and hearing my own voice and no longer requiring guides. But I was finding this part of the journey overwhelming and exhausting. When I had returned from my donkey trek and felt incredible, I had said to Christopher how rewarding he must find his work if he got such results. His reply was "I can't do this with everyone. I can only do this with people like you." I knew that once again this was another obscurity that I needed to find the answer to and if I didn't, only then would I ask him what was different about people like me? I contemplated these words over a long period of time. Was it because I had not taken the conventional route and my body was less

Chapter 12 - Detachment

contaminated with toxic radiation and chemicals? Was it because I had taken the choice of my treatment out of someone else's hands and not gone for the 'quick fix' but owned the responsibility of it myself? I couldn't answer this conundrum either. To own every step of this disease as being yours is a very hard and painful path and reversing it is even harder especially when everyone else thinks you are crazy and following a sure road to death. I thought about the remarkable man Alan Turing who, against all odds, broke the Enigma code, which probably shortened what would have been an even bloodier war by at least 2 years during which time another 14 million people might have been killed. Society 'honoured' him by chemically destroying his amazing mind and body because they could not make him 'normal' according to the conditioning of the majority at that time who believed that because he was a homosexual, he was a danger. Two of my favourite quotes of his sprang to mind:

"Sometimes it is the people who no one imagines anything of who do the things that no one can imagine."

"Those who can imagine anything, can create the impossible."

Was I really crazy in thinking that I needed to go back to 'mind' to find an answer? I had TWO very big reasons as far as I was concerned. My EMOTIONS were blocked by pain from being abused and unloved, rendering me incapable of receiving or giving LOVE. SPIRITUALLY I was closed down from FEAR of being told my ability to see into other dimensions and other possibilities was a form of madness and if they were to get out of control would then require long-term psychiatric treatment. Today I have the advantage of seeing I am not alone in my 'madness'. I can go to the internet and explore what an out-of-body experience is, what Qigong is, the collective consciousness and the smallest particles of the universe. But forty years ago, there were only my 'special' books I had hidden away. If these two very important aspects of my life were shut down, realistically what purpose was there for living? I slowly allowed myself to return to the word 'detachment'. It didn't mean detach yourself from the world and no longer 'feel' - quite the opposite. If one allowed oneself to experience an emotion fully but not become obsessed with it - like unrequited love or an obsession with acquiring something - then there was no pain attached to it. It is like a mother's love for her wanted child when first she lays eyes on it in the first minutes of birth. This beautiful 'unconditional' love is exactly that - 'unconditional' and 'pure'. There is no need to detach because it simply flows, because you are in each other's energy, part of each other - a sharing rather than a neediness. It is given willingly without any attachment to the outcome or needing to receive anything in return. It is infinite, unconditional and divine just like my journey into the void and the understanding of infinity - no beginning and no end. It meant feeling the emotion of love but not turning the key on it, locking it into the very core of your being and attaching it to you so that if others did not meet your expectations you felt wounded by it. Who are we to have expectations of others? They are our expectations, not other people's. Naturally we will feel hurt if other people don't give us what we are expecting of them.

I came across this beautiful piece in *Ramtha* which helped to clarify these thoughts:

"You create for yourselves a life of limitation by accepting limiting beliefs, which then become steadfast truths within your beings and thus the reality of your lives. You separate yourselves from life by judging all things, all people and even yourselves. You live by a code of fashion called beauty and surround yourselves with things that permit you to be accepted by the limited consciousness of man, which accepts nothing but its own unattainable ideal. You are babes who are born to grow up, lose the vitality in your bodies and believe yourselves into old age until you perish."

Slowly, I began to understand. In order to bring about changes in my physical body I had to detach myself from all limiting beliefs. Start again, like the primordial child. It wasn't just about the DNA but back to the zero point and to no concepts about anything. There was nothing, only pure consciousness, no judgemental belief system to lock into the cell memories, which causes distortion of mind and body if these belief systems are not processed and accepted as misconceptions about ourselves. Only by entering zero state, the original energy form of self, could you receive clear messages from spirit, otherwise how would you know that this was not ego or conditioned personality interfering. As my understanding grew, so the confusion I had created diminished. My paranoia about my beautiful journey being spoilt was my own limiting egotistical beliefs at play causing resentment and anger. This was above all what I needed to detach from, along with any fixed outcomes such as the one I had had in my treatment session. My fixed outcome was that I would go higher than ever before, but clearly this would not happen until the time was right. It would require careful observation and monitoring of these limiting emotions and then a release of them to allow love, the universal spirit, to flow into and through me. After all, it was my quest to go beyond what everyone else believed that had started

Chapter 12 - Detachment

this amazing journey in the first place. Rather than lack trust and dissolve into anger, it was time to be deeply grateful for the Haven and the extraordinary person that was treating me during this time who had not fixated on a cure for my cancer but more an expansion of the mind in which all things then become possible.

As I became calmer and more peaceful, I resumed Qigong and meditations. My meditations were now of flight and it was around this time that I had a reiki session with Sally, during which I could feel myself looking down on a beautiful flowing river and, as it meandered, I joined it like a bird flying above it and following its course. My outer world also reflected peace and calm and I continued to write, gathering information and reflecting on the courses I had delivered over the years to women's groups. It was time to pass this information on so others could also be trained to teach it. I had again found a purpose.

Summer was drawing to a close and in early September an opportunity presented itself to do a trek, to raise funds for the Haven. Nothing too strenuous - it was trekking Hadrian's Wall, which cuts through the Northumberland National Park. Starting at Lanercost Priory, the walk was 25 miles (41 km) alongside the only remaining sections of the wall allowing one to admire the scenery and the ancient monuments to be found along the way. It sounded perfect, just what I needed to set me up before the winter, and two weeks after the trek I would be starting my Qigong training.

I arrived at Haltwhistle station late in the afternoon of 9th September. On the country train I had met with a fellow trekker who had been told that I would be on the same train. As there were not many people and both of us were sporting rucksacks, Rochelle quickly made the connection with me. It wasn't long before we were chatting as if we had been lifelong friends. She too was on the non-conventional path of treatment. I felt at long last I was no longer alone and I knew that we had travelled all that way not so much for the trek but to simply make the connection with each other. As we got down from the train, we were met by the guides who were operating our trek. It was a rough, windy, wet, cold and bleak night and did not look promising for the days ahead. We arrived at Winshields Farm campsite and fortunately set up for us were about 10 little individual pod-like tents. I had brought a torch as sometimes I like to read into the night if I can't sleep so I was relieved to see that I would not be disturbing anyone if this was what I wanted to do, given that we were camping and I had not slept on the hard ground for many years.

Cancer - A Magical Quest

We were met with a delicious nourishing supper and a brief on what the next two days ahead were about and I felt confident that after Peru and the donkey trek this would be a pleasant, easy walk if the weather would only be kind. The night in the tent proved to be interesting. The wind howled and the rain lashed but inside the tent I was warm, dry and comfortable even if I could not sleep. I was grateful that I had not pitched the tent as I don't think it would have sat there robustly until morning. All credit to our tour guides, who were clearly expert in their field. Eventually I must have slept and woke to my alarm clock telling me it was 6.30 a.m. and time to make a move. Our planned time of departure was 8 a.m. Surprisingly, after such a night, the sky was showing a glimmer of hope and although there was a sharp wind it looked as though the day might turn out to be dry. In all the treks I have ever done I have never done one in the pouring rain and I hoped this would remain the case. After a warm shower, a generous breakfast and our rucksacks filled with our rations for the day, we were ready to pick up the trail. The most beautiful part of the morning for me was that standing in the doorway of the kitchen where we went for our food was a pony. No one seemed to be bothered that he just appeared and looked in at everyone and then accepted a cuddle from each of us. It settled me and made me feel at home as I was missing Iona and wondering how she would feel when each day went by and I did not appear. We had hardly ever been separated from each other apart from my Peruvian holiday.

The day turned out to be beautiful, warm and sunny with enough breeze to make a comfortable hike. Rochelle and I teamed up for a while and as we chatted, we realised that our lives had so much more in common than ill health and choosing a similar path for our treatment. We began our trek after being taken by coach to Lanercost Priory and walked our way mainly on small roads which passed through several small villages. Gradually we made our way to the ridge running alongside the Wall. The climb up to the Birdoswald Roman Fort proved to be quite steep and it took me a while to get my breathing into the right rhythm for the ascent. As the day wore on, I walked and chatted with other members of our small group, sharing stories about our diagnosis, our various treatment sessions at the Haven and our hopes for the future. It became clear to me as we chatted that my experience of treatment was unique and best kept to myself. It was enough that I was able to be with others and was again enjoying that feeling of being out in the open. As the day warmed up, I shed the layers of clothes until finally my exposed arms were able to absorb the benefits of the sun and

Chapter 12 - Detachment

the warm breeze. Within me I was content and just happy to be alive. We stopped for lunch at the Royal Army Museum and then continued our walk along the visible sections of the Wall following some breathtaking cliff tops and countryside. It reminded me of a giant and beautiful patchwork quilt of various shades of green divided into sections by grey stone walls and very similar to the countryside of the west coast of Ireland. Finally, we made our way towards the Cawfields Quarry and home once again to Haltwhistle having covered approximately 24 kilometres. Our very welcome campsite and supper awaited us. I felt tired in a healthy way and slept like a log that night in spite of the hard ground. Although this wouldn't be everyone's idea of recovering from cancer, for me it was of paramount importance to test my physical strength by walking, breathing clean air and being back with the smell and beauty of nature. A trek is like a pilgrimage for me. It is not only healing but generally takes me up a level to a new spiritual height.

Next day again proved to be ideal hiking weather, even hotter than the day before. After breakfast we climbed back up to the ridge and walked east beside the Wall. Our path took us along the Sycamore Gap to take pictures of the beautiful sycamore tree which had become famous and was awarded 'Tree of the Year' after its appearance in the film *Robin Hood, Prince of Thieves*. We then passed several lakes on the way to Housesteads Roman Fort, where we stopped for lunch. From here we continued to hike for a couple of hours towards our finish at Brocolitia and the Roman Temple to the sun god Mithras.

There had been some concern about finishing the trek before 5 p.m. as my train home was at this time and we had 17 km of fairly steep terrain to follow that day. There was talk about me being picked up by car at the nearest road point and taken back to the train station. However, quitting a trek is not in my rule book. We left a bit earlier than the previous day and as the day became warmer and the group energy gathered momentum, we arrived back with hours to spare even having time to pose for our group photographs at the finish point. Our guides had also brought along some bottles of Champagne to toast our success. We then boarded our waiting buses and returned to the campsite where I had already packed my rucksack for home. It had been a beautiful weekend made even more complete by sharing traumatic events with people who understood how much a cancer diagnosis can change everything as you become aware of how fragile time and life on earth really are.

This trek had had one more especially significant event for me. On the last day, while three fellow trekkers and I were walking through a field, a herd of cows quietly grazing in the field decided to make a move towards us. I was the person closest to them when suddenly the cow in the front decided to gather speed. I would not have been able to run away as my companions did because it had focused its attention very firmly on me and was bearing down with speed. Somewhere from my deepest memory bank was the phrase 'stand your ground'. So I did and pointed my walking pole firmly at it. The cow was not fazed and I thought should I lie down, but the chances of being trampled were high. As if from nowhere my intuitive voice stated:

"*Use sword fingers and stare it straight in the eye with intention and say the word STOP very firmly and loudly.*"

I did not hesitate, I carried out the act, and the cow ground to a halt just beside me, lowered its eyes and sheepishly turned and walked away. My fellow trekkers were watching from a distance and, when I joined them, they thought this was amazing and was a trick I had clearly used before and must be a dab hand at dealing with stampeding cows since I was from the country. I informed them that this was not the case and they decided that I was extremely lucky and told our guides about it when we met up with them. I realised that this was an affirmation of the power of Qigong. I had been attending my weekly lessons of 'Dragon and Tiger' Qigong for some months now and had been taught a particular hand movement known as sword fingers, which channels the energy very strongly and much more specifically to a point. I had been 'instructed' in this potentially dangerous situation to use it with 'intention'. This was a new concept for me - to target something with meaning and purpose directed by the mind. It gave a new power to what I needed to do within my body and its cells. I already knew how to look at my cancer cells in meditation and I knew how to move the energy within my body and up and down the meridians as described in Chinese medicine and acupuncture but I had not yet made the connection of using the mind to direct my own powerful energy into the very cells by intention. If I could stop a cow in its tracks by using Qigong, what could I do inside my own body?

I set off in the late afternoon back on my train journey home, filled with a new sense of purpose and excitement. My lessons of detachment had been long and arduous and hopefully now at an end. But the worst was yet to come. On arrival home, my beautiful Iona was so pleased to see me but I sensed and could instantly smell that there was something

Chapter 12 - Detachment

not quite right with her. During the summer she had developed ongoing gut problems and nothing seemed to be able to put it right. She had had several courses of antibiotics and had even continued them while I was away. Back in July she had been particularly poorly and because it was summer and quite hot, I had not noticed quite how much her consumption of water had gone up. The next symptom I noticed was when she finished her evening meal, she would take her paw and kick her food bowl around the floor and bark loudly and incessantly. She was demanding more food and Iona was not a dog motivated by food or treats normally. This makes Red Setters more difficult to train because they are motivated by fun, excitement, smells and activity rather than food. It took a while to track down what was happening for her but eventually she was diagnosed with Cushing's disease usually caused by a benign tumour in the pituitary gland but having a direct effect on the endocrine system of the body, in particular the adrenal glands. Occasionally, the tumour is in one of the adrenal glands itself and then more prone to being malignant. It is apparently very unusual to see Cushing's disease in such a young active dog. She was only seven and it is more associated with overweight, elderly dogs and is also unusual in Red Setters. I had a horrible feeling come over me. My pain had started in my adrenal glands. My dog had been living exclusively in my stressed energy. From my acupuncture sessions I was understanding that we are all connected and share the same consciousness and energy fields. Had I been responsible for her disease? Much later I was able to ask this question from her homeopathic vet with more than thirty years' experience of working holistically with dog and owner together. He remarked exactly the same thing. Frequently, over years where chronic illness was concerned, a dog would take on board similar ailments and conditions that its owner had.

This was now the biggest test of detachment. My dog had been not only my loyal friend but my closest companion throughout my seven years with her. As my young son jokingly said:

"*It's difficult to know where you and the dog begin and end.*"

And he was right. We lived in the most beautiful symbiotic relationship, the kind that had never been described in my school biology books but is the best description of symbiosis I know. I fed her, ran with her, cared for her and loved her and in return she gave me what everyone is searching for, that magical 'unconditional love'. She had been there for me through the lonely nights when I was coming to terms with dying. Her warm body with its silky fur nestling close to me, transferring comfort and love. Her warm tongue on my face asking me to get up in the morning for our run together as if she knew I needed to fill my stagnant body with oxygen, deep into my lungs. Even when I was struggling to get out of bed with the side effects of Arimidex, she would pull the covers off the bed and bark loudly as if to say 'we are in this together'. The thought of losing her was more than I could bear and was not one I was ready to face at all. She was my best friend. I checked out the medication for this disease and the side effects were as gross as chemotherapy for humans.

My search was about to begin again and I was struggling with keeping my heart from shutting down. I could not imagine life without her. If she had been old and had lived her life to the full, I could have accepted this a little more easily but she was a young vibrant dog. She ran the fields with me and in her mischievous way she would disappear into woodland for a full ten minutes or more. I would shout her name at the top of my voice, calling out like a fish wife, and eventually way ahead of me she would appear, sporting a head full of greenery as if she was carrying out an army combat exercise. Not a day went by that she didn't make me laugh. The reputation that Red Setters have of being a little mad is not wrong. She displayed her joy for life in whatever form it took, totally uninhibited and with little understanding of conditioning and discipline. It was these very qualities that I loved in her. I could not put her on medication that was unacceptable for me to take, let alone her. I searched for someone trained in complementary therapy for dogs and found Shelley in Andover in Hampshire. Only 30 minutes' drive from my home. She also carried out acupuncture for dogs. She saw Iona very quickly and organised to send me a bottle of herbs (similar to those found in Essiac tea used by me in the early days to cleanse and support my immune system). She made the potion herself adding specific ingredients depending on the dog's condition. She decided a session of acupuncture may also be useful. I was prepared to at least try something that was working so beautifully for me.

There is another important aspect to a dog or pet that only people who have suffered abuse in life will fully understand. The love is more profound because when you have been so hurt by people then trust is a huge issue. It is only in a loving relationship with an animal that this trust can again slowly be re-built. It is for this reason that therapy dogs are now being used for ex-soldiers who suffer from post-traumatic stress disorder and the same should be offered for all people who have this particular disorder, anxiety or panic attacks caused by human trauma. A

Chapter 12 - Detachment

close companion can help overcome so many otherwise insurmountable difficulties. Training dogs that need re-homing and placing them with ex-soldiers who have suffered trauma answers a need and brings a solution for both parties. Both understand what each other have gone through.

The end of September was fast approaching. Not my favourite time of year as it heralds the approach of winter, which is always my most difficult time of year. In England, this means several months of colder weather and shorter days. I was going to need my Qigong to activate and motivate me. On 24th September I set out early for London to meet my new teacher, Thalbert, and eight fellow students. We began by learning the basic Qigong standing exercises and started with the Earth element which is grounding and strengthens the body. We did flowing exercises, which were then balanced with static poses. The concept of Yin and Yang was explored and its place in balancing the mind and body. We were offered several representations of earth to choose from in order to focus our mind on earth as we entered into meditation. I chose a cave and as I closed my eyes, I could see myself entering a cave along with a large bear. There in front of me was a wall covered in cave paintings. I instantly knew that this was linked with the cave paintings in the meditation I had seen more than twenty years ago when I had attended Ruth White's courses with Tricia. We had been asked to 'see' what we had to give to the world and here was another piece of my puzzle – I now knew that cave paintings were more than depictions of the ancient people's daily lives, they were shamanic art.

My second day was even more eventful. As I practised the more expansive exercises, I closed my eyes to focus more clearly on what was happening within my body. In a flash, I was back in a life where I could see myself as a small boy of seven or eight. I was dressed in white clothes. My head was shaved and I was kneeling preparing vegetables for a group of men who looked like monks. They were dressed all in white with black tie belts around their waists. They were calling instructions to each other and were drawing something on the earth with a stick. I had been given strict instructions not to watch anything they were doing. Consequently, my place of work was in front of them so if I were to do the forbidden thing and turn around then they would see me. This did not stop me from listening and so one evening I went to my hut and tried out what I had heard. The head monk caught me and I was pulled roughly out of my hut and taken to the edge of a nearby mountain. He then told me that if I thought I knew so much, I should fly from the top of the mountain. He carried on goading me and took me closer and closer to the edge and instructed me to fly. I do not know whether I was too proud to apologise and beg for my life or too afraid to question him. I went to the edge and threw myself off. Naturally, I did not fly and that was how my life as that small boy ended. It seemed I already had some memories connected with Qigong and now was my time to re-awaken them.

CHAPTER 13

Initiation: Entering into Light

Following my first weekend sessions in Qigong it was expected that we not only practise the exercises taught to us but that we should keep a diary and observe what was happening within our bodies and minds as we practised. The main problem I had when I did the opening exercises that transform our basic jing was that I would feel extremely nauseated. The energies that are worked on in Qigong are referred to as the three treasures: jing, qi (chi) & shen. Jing is housed in the lower dan tien, an area which lies just above the pubis and approximately three fingers' width below the naval. Jing can be likened to an earthly or sexual energy rather like crude oil and is the most densely vibrating energy. In a series of exercises referred to as 'bringing up the jing', jing is transformed and refined first into chi and then shen. Chi is often initially felt in the hands which act like receptors for this refined energy.

The mind and body function as a result of the interaction of vital substances. These vital substances are known as substantial or material such as blood, essence (jing) and body fluids. The mind and spirit are insubstantial or immaterial, without form. Chinese written characters depict the insubstantial as steam and the substantial as rice. In a healthy body, ideally the energy should be directed by the insubstantial shen and not the body dictating how the energy is used. However, in the Western world our basic jing energy tends to dictate our lives, which results in a craving for food, alcohol and sex with an ultimate decline and destruction of the body.

When this nausea continued for several days, I felt that I was stuck in the jing energy, unable to move myself to the next level. I found that

I wanted to return to old unhealthy patterns of eating and I craved chocolate and sugar and generally felt the desire to repeat old coping mechanisms that were no longer appropriate to my changing and evolving life. I also noticed the recurrence of especially sharp pain in the adrenal areas when running for a train. Before falling ill, I had lots of these warning signs in my body which I had chosen to ignore. I also had problems in swallowing as though there was a permanent lump in my throat. In Chinese medicine this is referred to as 'plum stone throat' as if there is a feeling that a plum stone hasn't been swallowed properly and is sitting at the back of the throat. In Western medicine it is frequently associated with anxiety states and known as 'globus hystericus'. Chinese medicine, because it looks at the whole body, links this condition with a stagnation of energy in the liver area often caused by stress and creating other symptoms such as acid reflux and an unevenness in bowel function. I remember my mother describing the same feeling when she was ill. She described it as her 'craw'. Interestingly, this word means 'throat' and the phenomenon got worse when she was undergoing radiotherapy. She was prescribed antacids to deal with it but once again no one looked at the root cause. She particularly experienced it after eating sweet foods such as biscuits and chocolate and maybe it was her body's way of saying:

"You are poisoning me."

Could this be a reason for my nausea and old patterns of poor eating resurfacing? Was the Qigong releasing old cell memories of severe stress and a liver in a poor state from bad diet. I could also feel a tightness in my upper back as if my lungs needed to expand more. As I struggled with theses physical symptoms my intuitive voice made itself heard:

"*You need to go for an acupuncture session.*"

It had been more than three months since my last treatment and if I was being instructed to go back for a session then clearly there was a reason. I texted and booked an appointment for 13th October.

It was a beautiful meeting, made all the more lovely because now I had no expectations of what the meeting was to bring. My lesson had been learnt. No expectations and no concepts. I explained my physical symptoms and I asked the question that up until now I still had had no answer for:

"What was different about me?"

There was a pause for a moment and then Christopher replied:
"You listened."

Chapter 13 - Initiation - Entering into Light

No complicated jargon, just simplicity. As I pondered these words, I understood. I had listened with my entire mind and all the senses of my body. I received the acupuncture both visually and with a deep sense of 'knowing' and 'intuition' as he worked with me. I not only 'listened' with the whole of my body, I had learnt slowly and patiently how to decipher the language of symbols and riddles. It was never easy to fully comprehend what I was being told and that was the very nature of such instructions. I would need to spend time thinking it over, sometimes for weeks or even months and discussing it with Agnieszka. I had worked with everything my intuition had told me, from my diet, the books to read, what was happening inside my body, to my mind's ability to travel and bring back information. It was 'listening' but not just with my ears. But it had not just been down to me alone to listen. My orator was an exceptionally gifted communicator who had enabled me to listen.

While I was preparing for acupuncture, we discussed Iona and her care, detachment from situations and bringing an end to the current situation of what was making me feel sick. The situation was explained to me that if I felt physically sick then it meant that my body did not even want to try to digest something, it wanted to remove it completely by vomiting. Although these patterns may be seen as addictive, particularly the food addictions, there is no such thing as addiction. I would agree with this. There may be a slight physical addiction for example to the nicotine in cigarettes. But in the past, I had stopped smoking overnight. It was the 'thinking' that had caused the so-called addiction. From the thought comes the emotion, for example the false sense of cigarettes being relaxing. All that is relaxing in reality is the deep breath on inhaling all the toxicity from it. In fact, when one first smokes, there is a sense of light-headedness and often nausea as the toxins hit the body. Generally, if we stopped after that first cigarette, we would not continue. But it is this emotional connection that drives it. The mind and emotions tell us that we are feeling calmer; we are treating ourselves to some time out; relaxing away for a moment from the daily turmoil; allowing us to deal with our stresses. This habit has a ritualistic pattern to it, embedding it in the thought patterns that this was in fact a pleasurable and, in bygone days, a social way to relate to others. I stopped smoking overnight by changing the habits and thoughts that went with the cigarette and thereby altered the desire for one. I no longer associated it with a cup of coffee or a drink at the bar. I reprogrammed my mind by telling it that the toxins from a cigarette were disgusting, wrecked my health and smelt foul, and by doing this I made new neural pathways relating to smoking. Gradually then the old pathways disappeared because they were no longer being used, rather like weeds growing again on an unused path.

I also understood that I was being given this information about addiction for another reason. One can be addicted to doing things out of a 'sense of duty' which in fact changes nothing and could escalate a situation even further. Hence there is no point in feeling a compulsion to 'help' in a situation particularly if it is coming from a place of resentment. Unless people are prepared to change themselves, there is no point in 'rescuing' them until they desire this change for themselves. We have a choice over our behaviour and conditioning, we are not determined by it. If we choose to be in victim mode all our life and escape into this pattern rather than break from it, then others will see and treat us as a victim. This piece of knowledge was as pertinent to me about my own treatment sessions as it was to the people I was interacting with in my life at this time. I was on the cusp of making the most important changes of my life and yet I was held back by fear and conditioning. These exercises in Qigong would liberate my mind to a point where there was no way back, no return to the old ways of thinking because I would no longer be 'thinking' from just my bodily existence. A whole new ingredient and concept would be there, that of spirit or universal energy.

As I lay with the acupuncture needles inserted, this time with additional ones placed in the area of the pineal gland, otherwise known as the third eye, and another at the top of my head, just back from my forehead, I felt a beautiful sense of calm wash over me. As I closed my eyes, I heard a voice saying:

"Take off your shoes and socks."

These were my usual instructions before an acupuncture session. But this time it had a much more profound meaning. This is what one does in the East when entering a spiritual place of worship. I was familiar with this practice in Hindu and Buddhist temples when travelling through India. For me it represented not only leaving behind the dirt from the streets outside when entering a sacred place but also connecting with the earth energy through my bare feet when focusing on deity energy. As I settled myself, I heard a shrill, high-pitched whistle similar to that of a bird sound. I had no idea what this was as I had never heard such a sound before. As I listened, I was travelling up through the colours associated with the chakras of the body. First, the bright red sacral colour that reminded me of my fire element session. Then through orange,

Chapter 13 - Initiation - Entering into Light

yellow, green, blue and then speeding rapidly through pale and deep purple. Finally, I found myself outside what appeared to be a beautiful old, oval oak door. The hinges were solid and black like that of a medieval castle door with a thick round cast iron handle, the type that you have to slip your fingers through in order to grip and turn it. It reminded me of the small magic fairy door that I have on my bedroom door at home. From under the door glowed a bright, yellow light. I was instructed to enter through the door, taking care to close it behind me. As I entered, the golden light was dazzling, blinding even. I closed the door behind me as instructed and as I turned there was a row of faces before me which bore a resemblance to ancestors from different cultures. As my eyes focused on their faces, I began to see them as shamans. First, to my left was the old wizened, lined face of a North American Indian chief. He was wearing his full ceremonial head dress. I recognised him as 'White Eagle'. This was the name I had given him when I first met him as a spirit guide, many years ago in Ruth White's workshops. This period of my life began shortly after the workshop of the power animals and I had been shown the eagle as my power animal. The North American chief had been my guide for many years and was often quite harsh with me when I had not meditated and entered my inner world for many weeks. When I came back to it, he would admonish me and tell me in no uncertain terms that I had been away from my practices for too long. I was also much more deeply familiar with this culture. Many years previously when I was engrossed in past-life regression work, I had attended a one-day workshop in Exeter in Devon. In this session we were encouraged to regress to an appropriate life that our mind needed further clarity about. We were instructed to imagine we were flying above the world until we felt an affinity to a particular country. It was not long before I 'arrived' in North America. I had regressed to a male Indian chief who had gone to negotiate with another tribe to try to quell the tribal warfare that was threatening the lives of my tribe. On my return I found the whole tribe had been slaughtered in my absence. Such a sense of hopelessness washed over me and I recall my last words from that life as I killed myself:

"*There was nothing I could do.*"

I pondered again these words and wondered why I needed to remember them.

Standing next to the North American Indian chief was an Indian Saddhu, dressed in orange robes with a long white beard and a bright marking over his third eye. Saddhus are Hindu religious, ascetics who have renounced their worldly life and are well practised in yoga and meditation. For me he represented the ancient mystical culture of India which I had been privileged to discover during my early married life. Of particular importance were the chakras of the body, the gods and goddesses of Hinduism and Buddhism, and meditation. Beside him stood an oriental gentleman with long dark drooping moustaches either side of his mouth. He was dressed in a beautifully embroidered, sparkling red, gold and green jacket with matching cap. He appeared to be from China but I had never seen him before. I suspected he was depicting to me my new discovery into the Chinese practices of mysticism. I had studied some tai chi over the years at my local sports centre so I was already familiar with the flowing movements of this art. Now this was to go much deeper than the physical exercises. Finally, was Carl Gustav Jung, the founder of analytical psychology. His work had always fascinated and inspired me because he based his understanding on so many things - anthropology, religion and philosophy, and was known above all for his theory of the collective unconscious. I feel Jung has yet to be 'discovered' and was very overshadowed by Freud's thinking, which reflected and fitted with the Victorian era. As is often the case, those ahead of their time are frequently dismissed and only given full recognition many years after their death when the world is ready for their thinking. All of these figures standing before me in the light were important to me, particularly the ancient mystical practices represented by the first three. The last figure, Jung, in his lifetime had attempted to piece all of these things together and the author Hermann Hesse had also been greatly influenced by his way of thinking. For a brief moment I became aware of my physical body, and my feet felt as though an electric current was passing through them. The thought crossed my mind as to how I would stand on them later as these vibrational levels increased. As the figures stood before me, I was bathed and washed in a light so strong, so beautiful and so powerful. I felt as though I had been invited to an initiation ceremony. It was my own ceremony of my awakening. All the pieces of the puzzle had now been put together. All the knowledge, all the intuitive knowing throughout my life was being placed before me. It was as if I was being presented with the fact in vision form and was being told:

"***You have accumulated all this knowledge over this lifetime, what are you going to do with it now?***"

I thought of Sally, my reiki therapist's words to me after one of my sessions with her:

Chapter 13 - Initiation - Entering into Light

"Bring the ancient knowledge to the modern world in a way which people will understand it."

Was this the purpose of this lifetime? I wasn't sure. Clearly, I was being asked to prolong this life for a reason. With no conventional therapy, how was I even alive, let alone feeling so incredibly well physically and mentally?

All too soon the experience was brought to an end as Christopher entered the room and removed the acupuncture needles. As I went to get off the table, I struggled to put my feet on the ground, particularly the balls of my feet. I was aware of energy pulsing and throbbing through them. As I followed him down the stairs to the entrance hall, I again had a flashback to the life of the boy preparing vegetables for the monks teaching each other Qigong.

As I came out into the street from the Haven, it was a typical cold, dank, autumn afternoon and I hurried my way back to the Tube station. I marvelled at what I had just encountered. Such an incredible experience which left me overwhelmed with warmth, love and light. I was unable to comprehend why I had been chosen for this experience when there must be many more souls far more advanced than I was.

As always after such a session, things progressed rapidly. I was able to resume the exercises and noticed that I could feel my body releasing stiffness from the muscles, particularly in the shoulders and neck, and that my body was becoming much lighter as I walked. I wanted to press on a certain point on the balls of both feet which, as I studied more, I found to be an important energy gate of the body and very aptly named 'Bubbling Spring'. This was the very area which had pulsated when undergoing acupuncture. It was as if the gates had been opened as part of my initiation. As I practised these wonderful exercises, my body started to feel beautifully warm. This was a very strange experience for me, particularly warmth in my feet and hands, which felt frozen most of the time even on a warm summer's day. It showed me what poor health I had been in for many years.

Following my acupuncture session, I was also seeing the same silver chi in the air that I had seen by the sea when I was a child. As the flies readied for hibernation, I watched them 'dancing in and out' of the chi as they flew. Clearly, they were 'aware' of it. I was also becoming acutely concerned as to how the energy of others impact on us and particularly how they can both deplete and elevate our own energy. Of interest was the 'heavy' energy around people plugged into mobile phones. It was as if their energy field was being distorted and shrunken. They had no sense of lightness around them.

More importantly if we are all connected by the same consciousness this would explain how thoughts of hatred towards certain races and cultures could escalate to levels of war merely by thought alone. Therefore, what starts at one side of the world as a war could not be separated from the other side as we are all one. We share not only the planet, we breathe and share the same air and ultimately the same consciousness. The implications of this are enormous. It is the butterfly effect as suggested by Lorenz, that the flapping of a butterfly's wings might ultimately cause a tornado. If enough people even thought thoughts of hatred, without even voicing anything, it could escalate into war very rapidly, engulfing everybody in its wake. Imagine what world we would have if the thinking were reversed. What might humanity achieve?

Winter was fast pulling in and I was now ready for my second session of Qigong training. It was my favourite element, that of fire, associated with the colour red, the summer, the bird, and the heart. As we progressed with our jing and floor exercises, a new set of exercises was introduced called macrocosmic and microcosmic orbit. These are an amazing way of waking up the entire body and flowing your energy or chi throughout the meridians of the body. This was what Christopher had named in my third session when I had seen white light. These beautiful movements allow the body to take the crude energy of jing, transform it into chi and then finally expand and ascend it to join it with shen or spirit in order to energise the entire body. As we worked with entering that place of stillness or the void which allows the awareness of shen, I heard Thalbert make exactly the same shrill bird sound that I had heard in my initiation ceremony. I knew I was finally on the right path.

CHAPTER 14

The Halls of Illusion

By the beginning of December, I was beginning to practise regularly and learn to be patient with the years of stiffness that had accumulated in my muscles and joints. I listened to what was going on in my body and was no longer mechanically doing the exercises. That is the power that lies within Qigong. These movements cannot be practised robotically but they must first be felt and then gradually you become them, flowing with the rhythm that connects every cell to your body and your body to the universe. Although the purists would describe Qigong as 'energy work' I saw it very differently. For me it is a beautiful, ancient, shamanic dance with the elements, performed to generate and purify energy, with the lead role being taken by the heart, which houses the spirit. I could see my internal flow of chi and I could see that it was depleted in the left upper part of my body both front and back. I could see the stagnation in the left upper arm where the lymph drains from the left breast. It looked black and grey. As I worked through the fire element, I had visuals of a pyramid of light and the expansive bird exercise of crane spreading his wings and bringing release across my upper back. I felt a need to cough as I could see the stagnant chi begin to move rather like a dam that had not flowed in a long time. Bit by bit the channels were being opened and I realised that I had a choice whether to have cancer or not. In Chinese medicine, cancer is described as stagnant chi. In my case I thought of it as blocked emotions of self-hate, loathing, despair and depression all locked inside my cells and then compounded by abusive thoughts with a disgusting diet to finish it off with. This is something that Western medicine still has yet to understand. Experts think that it can be just cut out, hopefully getting all of it, so that you can get on with life in the same way without doing anything about the patterns of behaviour that caused it all. Even with very young cancer patients who may not be carrying these emotions for themselves, I wonder how much is in cell memories from grandparents and parents that they are bringing into their own life and how much also today's environmental factors are impacting on their will and ability to live.

As the cold of winter approached, I felt my body dip in energy and decided to have a further scan at the London clinic. This supposedly showed the tumour was getting larger and was without defined edges. I realised I now had to take radical new steps and not in the way of conventional therapy. I was still sure in my mind that this was not the way forward for me. I knew if I took this path, I would end my own life. It wouldn't need the side effects of the therapy to do this for me. I did more research and came across the work of Dr Pang Ming, a Qigong grandmaster and fully qualified Western style doctor of medicine. He had developed a medical Qigong known as Zhineng Qigong and was the director of the world's largest medicine-less hospital, the Huaxia Zhineng Qigong Centre, with its headquarters in Qinhuangdao, east of Beijing. The more I researched, the more excited I became. Here was Dr Pang's explanation for a supposedly incurable disease. "When chi gathers, matter appears and when chi disperses, matter disappears. So when chi gathers in an abnormal way, cancer appears and when the abnormal gathering of chi disperses, the cancer dissolves." According to Dr Pang, because chi contains information, it listens to our wishes. This would suggest that if chi listens to our wishes, we can command abnormal cells to disperse. This is what the teachers in the ChiLel Qigong Centre were showing students how to do. I went on to find a video of a bladder tumour being worked on by four teachers in the centre and being monitored by ultrasound by two Western trained doctors as the tumour went into spontaneous remission. Unfortunately, the hospital was closed in 2000 for political reasons.

The search for Dr Pang had taken me full circle to the Qigong school that I had originally thought about training with, run by Jeremy Colledge and his colleagues. The reason I had not chosen Jeremy's school was that I knew I needed first to go deeply into the five elements and finally alchemical Qigong. I sent a text message around the Christmas period to Jeremy and after some time elapsed, I decided that if I heard nothing back this was not meant to be. I was sitting quietly writing in my beautiful retreat and for a moment began focusing on what I should do for the future. Soon I would need to start work again as my pot of money which had aided my recovery was fast dwindling and I needed to keep a reserve. Suddenly, the phone rang and it was Jeremy. Rapport was so easy and I was able to talk about my quest but not really fully wanting to ask the question, 'can you remove the tumour as per Luke Chan's video of the removal of the bladder tumour in the Chinese Hospital?' I didn't know whether this was a possibility from Jeremy – having worked now with Qigong for more than 7 months and feeling the effects on my body of chi flow I didn't doubt that somewhere out there was someone who could carry this out. Part of me felt that maybe I was cheating by not removing this myself. I was certainly trying my hardest but I also realised that I was starting to lapse in my diet and exercise programme over the summer and that, if I expected someone else to take the responsibility for my dis-ease, this would not work long term. But I now needed help with how else to take these lumps of grief out of my body. I was able to see when I was practising Qigong exactly which meridians were blocked. I could see it as grey and black areas just like a stagnant smoky fog in my body. I could also see how much the right side of my body was trying to assist the left side by passing chi through the lower dan tien to the left side of the body. What an incredible repair system, I couldn't help noting.

I made an appointment with Jeremy for 24th January 2017 and, after a difficult train journey to Bath making me one hour late for my appointment, I was not quite sure what to expect. But I quickly learnt that making one at ease was something Jeremy excelled at. He picked me up from the train station and made a nice cup of warming herbal tea while I met the pets. Again, so different from the cold clinical and inhumane reception I had had way back at my hospital appointment. I can appreciate that this way is not for everyone but thankfully my conditioning, even in spite of my nurse's training, has not made me feel that the only way I can 'heal' my body is in a sterile environment where all emotions are kept carefully under anaesthetic. Nowadays, human touch in any form seems to be taboo as the human race becomes ever more politically correct to the point of being robotic, for fear of being sued for inappropriate behaviour. Jeremy's first introduction of a firm handshake was both comforting and reassuring. It made me feel as though I was in safe hands with my therapist. As Jeremy got further into the questions about what had led up to my diagnosis, I realised why I had struggled with my training session the weekend before. We had been working on the metal element, the organs for which in the Chinese system are lungs and large intestines and the emotion is grief – and, oh boy, was there plenty of that. It was probably most of what the tumour was composed of – thick, black, now-solidified grief that I had already explored before meeting Jeremy. I knew exactly what years this pertained to – it had all begun in 2008, the classic five to seven years before a tumour manifests to diagnosis point. As I travelled back in time again to those years, I could still feel the emotions deeply surrounding them. They had been relentless for me in terms of trauma – moving house, the loss of the children's private school fees, police involvement with the children, a tribunal for a job I had worked in for 14 years which showed me that loyalty meant nothing and money saving suddenly became all important. Then, the final job when I had spent my birthday in a meeting being told our options regarding yet another TUPE while my poor colleague had had to leave to cope with making the awful and sad decision to put her dog to sleep. And then finally there was my older son's motorbike accident in which his survival was nothing short of a miracle as I visualised a busy motorway on a dark, wet night and a lorry driver who just managed to stop in time. As Jeremy chatted with me, it all came to the surface and he was not wrong when he saw the lungs had been badly affected by grief. Maybe this is also the reason why metastases generally materialise in the lungs – not just because of the close proximity but because breast cancer is often associated with mother and mothering issues as was my case (left side) or father and marital home issues (right side) – all issues that cause grief and cause shallow breathing as you learn to suppress tears. As I spoke, I described it like Alice's pool of tears – that if I cried, I would not have been able to stop nor hold everything together.

'Diagnosis' dealt with, it was onto the 'operating table' in a beautiful room filled with light and plants and a cat that chimed in periodically with comforting purrs and deeper vibrational sounds that she may well have learnt from the environment she was living in. Jeremy systematically worked throughout the meridians, releasing as he worked. On the left side, as he worked on my hands, I had images of piles of ironing disappearing out through a window – this was how I had partly earned a living in the early days to pay for my children's school fees, working sometimes all night so that the clothes could be delivered the next morning as I dropped my children at school. Jeremy's way of working gave me a very strong earth energy, which was very grounding and in complete contrast with the middle (the heart) and upper dan tien (pineal gland and crown) energies that Christopher predominantly affects when

Chapter 14 - The Halls of Illusion

he works with me. It was interesting to note that Jeremy picked up how much Christopher's work with me had held my heart energy together, without which I would certainly not have been alive. By the time I had come to work with Christopher one year previously, I had already realised that if there wasn't some drastic intervention, I would be dead very quickly. I remembered how my face had been so sallow, lined and haggard with huge black bags under my eyes and in a 'Guess her age' competition, I would have easily passed for an eighty-year-old who had spent her life on the streets. How different I had looked and felt after two acupuncture sessions and a donkey trek.

Jeremy finished my session with the sound of a Tibetan singing bowl and I found the sound taking me into a visual spiral of vibration and my DNA was being incorporated into that spiral. I reached a new sense of awareness of what I had been given from my earth meditation in session four of my training. I had experienced the earth element through the five senses where I could see myself lying on grass in the mountains. These five senses were now being explained using visuals and sound and I understood why the elements are given a colour, a sound, a taste which in turn is linked with a smell and a feel, for example cold for the water element and heat for the fire element. My meditations and experiences were becoming integrated with my Qigong exercises which in turn were leading to liberation of mind and body resulting in a sense of wholeness and well-being. The sounds from the singing bowls were something I certainly wanted to investigate more, particularly when I later learnt that these bowls alter our brainwaves from a beta state to an alpha state and sometimes even theta. The theta brainwave range is the one in which the body and mind's natural self-healing processes are activated and optimised. They are present during deep relaxation, dreaming, meditation and hypnosis. How did these amazing people know all this without any 'scientific proof' of what was going on in the cells of the body?

I finally ended my beautiful session with exercises of La Qi and lung exercises to practise at home. Both are really powerful to rid the body of all forms of toxicity especially emotional. Jeremy suggested that I use the video of Luke Chan's bladder tumour dissolving but that I visualise a breast tumour instead and on the in breath bring the hands together with a visual of a perfectly formed breast and on the out breath the tumour being extracted. This visualisation worked well for me. I did not want to be 'fighting my cancer in any shape or form' - a war inside my own body when there is enough going on outside is not where I was at.

If I wanted a more fun version, I had a bunch of dancing cleaners doing a workout through the meridians to the song 'Shake it like a bee' by Francesca Maria. I realised as I did the lung exercises that in spite of my fitness through dancing, walking my dog and all my Qigong exercises, I was struggling to expand my chest out and contract it back down again for the depth of the exercise. Although Jeremy had suggested eight to twelve repetitions of these exercises, three times per day, I decided that I may have to take the pace more slowly and build up gradually. The important thing about visualisation techniques is to give them an energetic aspect. By imagining chi or energy and moving, it allows one's mind to expand to the possibility that the tumour is no longer solid and stuck and growing.

After my session had finished, I was again dropped back to the station and I felt that this was not the last I would see of Jeremy - yet again, another amazing energy worker had come into my life. As I made my way back home, I decided to stop off for my Zumba class to express my new 'lightness of being'. Most of my class mates have no idea what is going on in each other's lives but we all have a great deal of fun together and have formed a lovely friendship among the regulars - so when I turned up without my sports kit, we had a good laugh about my dedication to the class. When I got back home that night, I stood at the kitchen sink clearing the aftermath of the usual tsunami of dishes from the night before. I had had another amazing day but there would have been no point in sharing it. There was no one who would have understood. Both of my therapists had clearly seen and echoed each other with what was needed to bring about important changes in my life but my 'seer' Kristos had not seen an easy way out of this dilemma.

That night I went to bed early. I felt I had had a complete body workover at this stage and needed to sleep. I woke at 3 a.m. with such soreness exactly at the site of the larger tumour. It was a soreness as if the area had undergone surgery. This tenderness and soreness persisted for many days and even almost a week later I could still feel it. I did not feel worried - it felt like physical proof that Qigong was no spell and that something was once again shifting at the tumour site and that there was heat radiating from it. Over the coming days I had a busy work schedule which made any practice very difficult but I did my best and I could feel phlegm loosening at the base of my lungs that I was not even aware of previously. Also, remarkably, although I had been in a closed, stuffy room over the weekend with two of my fellow Qigong students who were clearly battling with the after effects of flu with much coughing and

Chapter 14 - The Halls of Illusion

sneezing, my immune system was holding up. I was supplying it with large doses, within the safe range, of slow-release vitamin C and D3, as well as with selenium and iodine supplements. I had previously stopped all my original supplements suggested by the nutritionist at the Haven but following my visit to Jeremy I decided to re-start them – probiotics, Candaway (to deal with the overgrowth of yeasts in the body, particularly Candida albicans) and Co-enzyme Q10, which acts as an antioxidant protecting the cells from damage. It is also involved in synthesising ATP, vital in fuelling the mitochondria of the cell which are responsible for cell repair and growth. The mitochondria use oxygen (aerobic) to drive this process but cancer cells are more primitive and obtain most of their fuel supply from sugars without the use of oxygen (anaerobic). In cancer it has been found that the mitochondria play a key role because the number and function of them are reduced. They are also responsible for triggering cell suicide (apoptosis), which is how the body normally gets rid of cells that it no longer needs. For good measure I also began my Essiac tea once more, which I had stopped when I had felt myself recovering. It is something I tend to do to my detriment – once I feel an improvement coming on, I relax and relapse into old ways. Jeremy followed up with an extremely helpful email going over everything we had worked on and added links with more exercises – now it was down to me once more to do the work and find the motivational push to take this to the next stage. Again, the unmistakable reminder was there that I had to be my own 'Medicine Buddha'. As I worked on myself the winter finally drew to a close. We were now entering into the time six weeks after the winter solstice where the nights begin to get visibly shorter. And, joy of joys, I had spotted the first snowdrops poking through the ground. It wouldn't be long before the crocuses appeared and then the daffodils and finally the warmth and long days of warm sunshine, once again returning to my time of year for creativity and energy flow.

I had made the link to the Chinese Medicine-less Hospital; I had received 'treatment' from an energising practitioner; and I could feel the physical proof that 'something' had very definitely happened at the main tumour site. I was now waiting for the next step as to where life would subsequently take me.

The next step was very close behind. It was now February 2017 and, shortly after seeing Jeremy, a physical and emotional situation that my son had created, and both of us had been carrying unhealthily for seven years, dramatically changed and altered his life for the better. However, I now realise that when you have carried a heavy load for so long it takes a while for the body and emotions to readjust and, some days after the news came, the right side of my body went into a mini crisis. As my emotions changed as a result of this news, so the right side of my body resumed its sharp stabbing pains in the adrenal areas associated with work and emotional stress before I became ill. Old ligament pains in my right shoulder returned as did sore, sticky eyes. I was in so much pain and discomfort but I now intuitively knew that it was old emotional baggage that needed clearing rather than anything sinister going on. I felt somewhat ashamed that this stuff was still resurfacing, having felt sure I had by now let go of it all, but clearing the body like the art of perfecting Qigong is an ongoing process.

Because of the pain and discomfort, I quickly went back for my eighth acupuncture session with Christopher in the same room with the skylight. It was not long before I was once again in a deep and profound meditation. This time it was a very strange one indeed. The scene was in black and white and gave me the impression I was in a theatre of illusion with people masquerading and portraying something they were not. Gradually, as I continued to watch, the black and white took on a coloured hue and then finally became full colour. Many different shapes and colours appeared, crowns of gold floated by, red cloaks worn by emperors, particles of things some of which fitted together and others that did not – all were swirling in clouds of mist. Then there were masks and people were choosing them, wearing them and exchanging them like a bizarre masked ball. They reminded me of a set of hand-painted Chinese porcelain masks that I owned. They had caught my attention some time ago in a charity shop – each one was unique with its own painted face. There appeared to me no real meaning to what I was seeing other than a feeling of being in a strange fantasy but then it took on an air of reality as people got more fully into their parts. I watched and was invited to participate but I had no desire at all to do this. I instinctively knew that this was all a charade. I wanted to have nothing to do with it and instead I felt as though my body was invisibly gliding through it to the other side of the room. As I looked back, a few people glanced after me as though they were aware I had moved through the room, but to the others I had been non-existent. It reminded me of how I had felt during most of my life. I often imagined when I was at discos with my friend that I was behind a two-way glass; I could see everything that was going on but nobody could see me.

I asked silently what this all represented and was told this is life here on the earth plane. There is no real meaning to the things we strive so

Chapter 14 - The Halls of Illusion

hard for and that seem so important at the time – they are in fact all an illusion. Learn the lessons while you are here, teach others what you have learnt if they want to listen, and free yourself. Far into the distance I could see the glow of a never-ending light like a bright full moon, constantly beckoning and always there but then the mists would come up and cloud over its glow similar to a dark rainy night on earth. I was given the explanation that eventually, when the theatre of illusion was finished with, only then could you reach the light, ready to finally let go of anything that emotionally held you attached to the earth plane and exchange the physical body for a light body in order to transcend into the light and infinity and finally from where we began this physical existence. I asked what the purpose of this journey was and the reply was ... to take the essence of the light you are given, grow it, share it and return to the light, having lit the flame for many others along the way so that eventually the glow adds to the eternal consciousness to then light the way for many others. The purpose is to raise human consciousness, both your own and others. Getting deeply caught up in human emotions along the way prevents the passage and confuses the path. Now for a second time I was asked the same question:

"*What do you want to come back for?*"

This time I answered differently. It wasn't just about my dog, it was about imparting the knowledge to others. I now understood that the main lesson of the past seven years – the lesson my son and the tumour had taught me – was compassion. This lesson was now at an end. I had finally understood and so closure was possible. Other life experiences were presented too. The purpose of my birth and the parents I was born to was to teach me that mind has the ability to overcome physical obstacles and even change aspects of the physical body. The abuse was to teach humility. The illusions of life such as wealth, physical earthly love, power, none of it has meaning unless the real purpose of the journey is understood, which is to return to the source having alleviated pain and suffering by opening your eyes to the illusions around you and focusing on unconditional love. The symbols I received were the Hindu goddess Green Tara of compassion, the mountain lion of leadership and a beautiful powerful white gyrfalcon ready for flight sitting high up on a mountain top alone. The gyrfalcon is the bird of kings and is highly prized. When I asked what it represented, I received the words:

"*True power can only come with compassion so use it gently and wisely.*"

At this point Christopher had already come quietly into the room and began removing the needles. I again had the sense that he knew exactly where I had travelled to in my meditation and this was only possible if we all shared the same consciousness which appeared to have different vibrational levels.

As I made my way home, I could feel such a lightness in my body and was once again in awe of how this ancient craft of acupuncture in the hands and mind of the right person could have such an intensely powerful effect. I have learnt to deeply respect Chinese medicine, which looks at every part of the person – mind, body and spirit, but also the environment we are in and how our senses respond to this. When Western and Eastern medicine are truly combined as equal approaches, there will be a phenomenal health system in place but the West has a lot of understanding to do and arrogance to let go of; meanwhile precious resources are being wasted as they wait for science to prove what the ancients already knew. An example of this is the Big Bang Theory which has been hailed as one of the greatest discoveries of our time to explain creation, and yet the Taoist creation story expressed a similar theory thousands of years before. The same theory, now revamped with a new name.

After a deep, dreamless night's sleep I woke the next day with no trace of any painful physical symptoms. I couldn't even remember where the aches and pains had been and I felt completely energised!

As I moved on to session five in Qigong, Thalbert happened to mention that when you view things from a higher level and see the greater perspective then you are more aware. This fitted in perfectly with the concept of illusion that I had been shown in my acupuncture session. Had I not been aware of the higher realms that I have been taken to, then I would not and could not have understood the illusion on the earth plane that we cling to so helplessly as if by trying to make it a firmer reality it makes life 'safe'. It is this very hope of making life safe that causes the restriction of the mind and ultimately our growth.

CHAPTER 15

Completion

As I pondered the 'halls of illusion' and the fact that one day I could feel such intense emotional and physical pain and the next day be completely pain free, I marvelled at this entity we call 'mind'. I also reflected more deeply on my journey. It had begun with the hope of finding an answer to healing my body from cancer. But my journey had very quickly turned into so much more. From session two of acupuncture and my trek with a donkey, my whole world and way of thinking had changed. I no longer feared anything, neither life nor death. I found myself in a place of just 'being' and living in the moment so that when your senses are fully in the moment, the next one takes care of itself. There is no hankering or longing for anything and when you give an 'idea' your thought and then follow that up with intention then it triggers the ability for it to happen. The secret is to let go of the layers of conditioning and beliefs undergone since birth so that you can become yourself and not what others think you should be; that is their perception of you, not yours.

As my Qigong course progressed and the spring gave way to warm summer mornings, I was awake early and practising the exercises with the windows open and the sound of bird song filled my body with its energy. The meditations I experienced were beautiful and frequently took me into travelling in light. I was now able to generate and experience for myself similar journeys into infinity which up until now I had only been able to do while undergoing acupuncture. This time I was flying solo. Physically, as my body was able to absorb more sunlight, I began to feel well and strong and I realise that for my future permanent well-being I will need to find a warm, bright environment to live in. As if to prove my new-found physical strength, my older son invited me to New York for a long weekend to celebrate his birthday. I jumped at the chance and, knowing my love for trekking, he suggested that on one of the days that we did a trek alongside the Hudson River. My son's apartment is on the 54th floor overlooking the Manhattan skyline. On my first day it was dull and overcast with the threat of rain for the whole day. I woke early and as I lay in bed on my first morning, I was able to watch the changing sky; as there was nothing else on the skyline and I was so high up, I felt much closer to this huge expanse. It made me think about the emptiness that I had experienced in the infinity of the void. It was just like the sky, ever changing. The clouds came and went, dissolving and changing shape and then a greyness developed until all around was a deep sense of entering into greyness and nothingness and finally stillness. Even then in the apparent stillness there is a sense of movement until within that greyness finally light filters through. Watching the sky helped me to think more clearly about what I had seen and how to express it. Imagine in the sky and clouds a different dimension to it as if you are looking at the sky in 3D with a pair of special glasses; and you can also see immeasurable amounts of tiny chi or energy particles jumping around in what appears to be random movements; and at the same time the clouds are moving and changing. These all exist in different energy forms and then there is the room that you are experiencing this all from. All are aspects of 'reality'. Outside the window everything is ever changing and moving, one minute, dense and grey, the next minute allowing light to filter through, next gathering for a storm and then clearing to allow blue skies and sun to appear; and the chi goes on moving and sparkling within it so this also is real for those who can see it. Trying to describe it is rather how divers must have felt when they went to the bottom of the sea for the first time and witnessed all the amazing fish and plants and sea creatures and then, without a camera, having to come back and describe to others what they had seen with only their words and memory to convey the information.

To take consciousness a stage further, visualise that you are looking down from 50 floors above at the buildings and roads below and at all the people and vehicles moving. They appear like small ants. Imagine that those down at that level only ever see their immediate surroundings at ground level. At another level there are those who look at the tall buildings around them and look in at the windows and occasionally look high above into the skyline. Then there are those living and working in these buildings and they have an awareness of this skyline every day. Above this are those living and working at the top of the buildings with the

Chapter 15 - Completion

awareness that there is the huge expanse of sky. Then there are those who are flying over New York seeing all of it before them. Finally, there are those few individuals who experience space flight, and for them their reality for a while becomes the existence of the cosmos. What lies beyond may also enter into their minds. For those on the very lowest levels of consciousness, they may not even be able to imagine what lies beyond. For them, the real physical world is all they may ever focus on life after life. Supposing in this vast expanse of consciousness is contained all the Akashic records belonging to everyone who has ever existed and our brain can filter this just as our lungs have the capacity to take in air. We all have a different capacity to take in air, depending on the size of our lungs and the efficiency of our respiratory muscles and then we have a different capacity to extract the oxygen and send this round our bodies and expel it along with the body's waste products into the atmosphere. We are also all connected because we are sharing the air that we breathe. What if this is also true of the brain, that our brains are doing the same thing as our lungs only instead of air, we take in consciousness? We all share this and each of us has a different capacity to process it and as we process it, we make it our own individual consciousness until we die. If our 'muscle' capacity is greater, we can experience more and to a higher degree. Just like the analogy of those living in New York City experiencing the different levels. If we limit the consciousness by conditioning and the day-to-day illusions of life of material requirements such as fast cars, bigger houses, more technology and consumer goods, then this will be our consciousness. Since we all share this consciousness and influence each other with it then this will be our collective consciousness also. We will then be 'trained' and conditioned to acquire more and more of this and have no ability to know that there is something higher than all of this because we are so focused on the so-called 'real' world. That is not to say that this is right or wrong, it is simply the level of consciousness that people are busy achieving now at this moment of our evolution. This particular era has to play out until humanity can move to the next level from Homo sapiens to Homo noeticus with a whole new awareness and understanding of our existence. However, it will require those living at a higher mental vibrational level to assist those living at a lower vibrational level to evolve the human race from war to peace, from poverty to enough for everyone, from conditional to unconditional love. Taking into consideration that each person evolves at their own pace, this may be a very slow process. If more and more people learn to take their minds to a higher level, connect with the universe and channel the light so that it becomes as much part of their lives as breathing – how much more incredible might this be than the virtual worlds being created for people by technology. At the present time, more challenging than any computer game is the ability to stay connected to the light and not return to old familiar patterns of conditioned behaviour when confronted by daily life with all its trials and tribulations.

After reflecting on this for some time, I decided to do my usual session of Qigong before starting the day. I marvelled that in such a short space of time this had now become a way of life for me, working and expanding my flow of energy and closing with meditation. In this way, I was learning to transition between the two worlds – the halls of illusion and that of my inner world of light and tranquillity.

Because of the rain, we decided to postpone our trekking until the next day and instead we toured New York City. Included in our trip was the Ground Zero Museum telling the tragedy of 9/11. It was so very sad looking at all the pictures of so many young people who had lost their lives that day in such a senseless act. Looking at the memorabilia collected from the scene it gave one the feeling of an eerie mass murder that had been committed that no one was ready for and no one could have stopped. My thoughts are never far from how fortunate I am to be alive. So after my trip the next day across the Hudson Valley, approximately 1,600 feet above the river, and after my particularly hair-raising descent down Breakneck Ridge when my son took the wrong path, I sent an email with a picture to Sonia at the Haven. I can never have enough gratitude to the staff of this wonderful centre. If only more people had access to these superb centres dotted around the country and at least have the opportunity to have a few sessions before choosing conventional treatment so that they are not making rushed decisions from a place of fear and depleted body energy.

On my return from New York it wasn't long before I had the chance to make a trip to Russia in the autumn. It was such a huge contrast between the two countries but I loved the city of Moscow, which at this time has no obvious ugly high skyline and retains much of its history and beautiful buildings. My outer journeys were very much reflecting what was happening in my inner world. Just as my New York trip had helped me to express what I had seen in infinity, so the Winter Palace at St Petersburg was very much a precursor of my final and ninth session of acupuncture to come. Entering the palace, one is met with the vibrant colour red and the overly ornate gold. It was on the one hand beautiful

Chapter 15 - Completion

and on the other overpowering. Each room of the palace seemed to just empty into the colour gold. I could not imagine how it would feel to live in this colour every day and sensed that perhaps there would come a time when the occupants would no longer 'see' it. Towards the end of my trip, I had a visit to a flamboyant evening of folk dance, music and song made all the more special by the exquisite display of the performers' embroidered costumes. Then came the grand finale. On the last night there was a visit to the Hermitage Theatre to see Swan Lake. I have always loved this ballet and no matter how many times I see it I always enjoy it. This was no exception and the theatre was so simple in its backdrops to set the scene that one was not so caught up in the settings, which is often the case nowadays as they become more and more elaborate.

Once back in England I again returned to my daily practice of Qigong which had lapsed during my trip to Russia. My ability to feel chi in my hands was increasing and I was frequently waking in the early hours of the morning with it pulsating in the palms of my hands. This was no hocus pocus as my children frequently called this type of phenomenon if I ever talked about it to them. If I could feel it flowing in this way... what did this mean? If I was feeling it then it existed for me, and if this was the case and I could activate chi, this meant I could do it in all the organs of my body including my breast. This energy, which I converted from basic jing to chi and then finally into shen, allowed me to travel in my mind into infinity. I felt sure if I could travel in such a way then it must be possible in my mind to transform this physicality of blocked chi in my breast into an energetic form. I had created it by thought and I now felt that, once and for all, I could de-create it. But how to do it?

The last vital piece was soon to be imparted to me. I was coming to the final part of my Qigong training, 'Developing the Yi'. Just as I was putting my quest together so my Qigong mirrored this and I was putting together meditation, breathing techniques, symbolism, visualisation and the final one - intention. When all of these are aligned it ensures that mind, body and spirit awareness are possible. Although I was practising regularly there was something that I needed to complete the flow for me. Autumn had set in and with it my sprit began to plummet. I could feel throbbing pains in my kidney area again and my life felt out of balance. As I aligned my body more and more, I realised that throughout my life I had never acknowledged the female aspect of me - from the child who was expected to be Patrick, to the adolescent who carried heavy loads of bricks for my father whenever any construction was going on in the home, to the adult who had learnt to be both male and female in the home but mostly male, parenting two boys. I was not sure how to bring about this balance in my body to finally accept I was Patricia and acknowledge the left side of my body both physically and emotionally and bring the fire element fully to life in all its creativity.

I knew that this needed a deep connection with myself and I could not do this with just my own practice of Qigong. I made an appointment for an acupuncture session for 9th November, two weeks before my completion of my Qigong training. Once again appeared that uncanny numerology - the 9th session on the 9th day. As I booked myself in at the reception desk, the regular receptionist recognised me and remarked she had not seen me for a long time. We began chatting and she asked me more about how I had done my cancer journey without conventional therapy. She assumed it was mainly diet change. I explained a little of what had been going on and how the role of mind had also played a large part and had always fascinated me. I found myself recounting my seeing the picture of the Tibetan monks in an encyclopaedia depicting them altering their physical body temperature by mind. We then chatted about acupuncture sessions and how amazing I found them and how I had been somewhat reluctant to even give them a try. It was more a last resort rather than having any high expectations. At that point, I sensed Christopher standing behind me and I turned to look at him. I had not had any treatment for nine months and we greeted each other like dear friends who had shared an extraordinary adventure together and now acknowledged it. There was such a warmth and deep respect for each other. I had been given the vital ingredients to be nurtured back to life by someone with years of ancient oriental skills and experience and I was living proof standing before him that something had caused me to survive against the medical odds. Like a master conductor, he had tuned the organs of my body until the whole orchestra was in harmony. I had then listened until I began to learn not only how these musical instruments worked in harmony but how every note that was emitted mattered. I now know that different organs of the human body produce different resonance frequencies. The heart resonance frequency is about 1 Hz. The brain has a resonance frequency of about 10 Hz; blood circulation about 0.05 to 0.3 Hz.

(https://phys.org/news/2016-10-scientists-effects-infrasonic-vibrations-humans.html#jCp).

The hertz (Hz) is the derived unit of frequency in the International System of Units (SI) and is defined as one cycle per second. It is named

Chapter 15 - Completion

after Heinrich Rudolf Hertz, the first person to provide conclusive proof of the existence of electromagnetic waves.

Along with the physical tuning of my body came the other two essentials, the mind without limitations and a spirit which could flow. Why, I ask, are we not taught as young children that our bodies are completely magical and sing their own song and when the song becomes out of tune, we need to find someone who can once again tune it for us before it becomes diseased? I have watched the effect that Tibetan singing bowls have on my body and also on that of my dog. I watch her respiration slow down until she is completely calm and at peace. I have witnessed the effects of acupuncture, Qigong and reiki on my body and Iona's and I am again astonished not only by what our ancestors discovered but also by our ignorance in assuming it has no worth. Most importantly, in this present day, these skills must be performed by authentic practitioners who can be trusted. This then allows for a true evaluation of these practices.

I followed Christopher into the lift and as we reached our usual top room with the skylight, I explained that I was now nearing an end to the first part of my Qigong training but that I was struggling with winter. He corrected me that it was autumn and then went on to explain what this might mean for me. As usual I had no need to explain anything. In a few sentences he had verbalised what the physical symptoms were all about without the need to address anything directly. Once the needles were inserted, I closed my eyes and entered into the stillness. I heard the door close and I drifted further into the silence. I could see my body lying on the table and then, from the top of my head at a point known in the meridians as Baihui down to a point at the perineum between the legs known as Huiyin, came a blade of light. It made me think of the legendry sword of Excalibur and it divided my body into right and left. On the left side appeared a ballet dancer in a skin-coloured leotard. She wore a pair of pink ballet shoes and there was an ethereal appearance to her as she danced and wove in and out of gossamer ribbons of blue, green, purple and pink light beams. Her body was completely soft and flexible and at times it was difficult to see whether she and the light were all one. As she danced, her hair came free and floated out behind her. It was long and dark and made me think of my long waist-length hair of childhood, which for me represented femininity. She was beautiful and what for me would represent the perfect depiction of the female. I was now drawn to look at the right side of my body. There was only the colour red in floating shapes and vague formations. As I looked at it, I associated it with power and strength and my beautiful fire element that made me feel happy and alive. As I continued to look, similar formations appeared in gold, bright, bright gold intertwining with the red and then separating out. It was as if these colours too were dancing in unison with my dancer on the left. Whereas one side was so soft, delicate and ethereal, the other was strong and bold, but neither overpowered the other. Both were important in order to enhance each other. It was the Yin and Yang in perfect harmony if I were asked to describe my perception of it. For me, my left female side would always be a dancer. On the male side, I understood the power and strength but not the ornate gold like I had seen in the Winter Palace. I asked what the gold represented as it became stronger and stronger in the visual. The reply I received was:

"*Seeing the Divine in Everything.*"

At first, I struggled with this. How could you always see the Divine in everything? I thought about my own abuse and those that I worked with on a daily basis who had suffered the most awful atrocities in their lives. How could one see the Divine in that? Slowly I was reminded about what was remarkable about these survivors. They could still love from their hearts even though they had been brought to the point of being broken. They still cared passionately, either for animals or other human beings who were suffering. That love never left them no matter what. Those females were like my beautiful delicate dancer. But what of the male side? For the most part in the world today it is out of balance, man ruling from a superior position, dominating the female, which can never create anything positive or beautiful and results in pain and suffering for everyone who comes into contact with him including ultimately himself. When male and female honour each other, together accepting each other's divine higher self, only then is there the possibility of perfect union and harmony on the earth plane. This Cherokee poem says it in its simplest form:

A woman's highest calling is to lead a man to his soul, so as to unite him with Source. Her lowest calling is to seduce, separating man from his soul and leave him aimlessly wandering. A man's highest calling is to protect woman, so she is free to walk the earth unharmed. Man's lowest calling is to ambush and force his way into the life of a woman.

Finally, my meditation came to a close with a small table on which sat a curious glass paperweight. Inside the glass bubble were some small figures of Tibetan monks sitting cross-legged with a background of snowy mountains behind them. It was like a child's Christmas snow globe.

Chapter 15 - Completion

Around it was a long string of wooden beads, a mala, the type used in Asia for reciting mantras. At the bottom of the mala was what appeared to be a clasp but that didn't seem to be appropriate for such a string of beads. To me it looked more like a little book.

I did not hear Christopher enter the room as I was still lost in thought. He quietly removed the needles and I slowly got up from the table. He showed me to the top of the stairs and I had a sense that this if not my last ever session, it would be my last for a long time. This was his way of showing me that I was now ready to do the next part of the journey on my own. I went down the steps on my own and I didn't look back. The falcon was ready for flight. The bird with the broken wing that I had been shown all those years ago in Ruth's workshop had been restored to wholeness. I was complete.

From the start, my journey through cancer was never about the quantity of time I would be given but the quality. If one is living in the past of remorse and living in the same negative patterns from childhood there can never be a quality of life and that is why cutting out, burning and poisoning the cancer could never be my path. I had to explore it, understand it, and above all come to terms with me, who had given birth to it. Somewhere along the way I had chosen to react to my abusive situation by depression and poor coping mechanisms and then trigger the ultimate destruct button which was the cancer gene passed to me on my mother's side of the family. I did not care for my body or my mind at that time. I did not know how to, nor did I even really know who I was anymore. I was caught up in the illusion of work, and the drama of the family and other people's lives, thinking that it was my responsibility to try to fix it all when ultimately it has to be our own. The Haven (now known as Breast Cancer Haven), so aptly named, taught me that. Each member of staff worked with me with such loving kindness that, at first, I did not know how to react. Slowly, I felt my life force return and as it did, it was to become the most magical experience of my life. I became aware of how my body really felt and my energy field and others around me. The depth of meditation I experienced was phenomenal. The numbers of years left on the earth plane was irrelevant because, as I had experienced, there is no beginning and there is no end. There is just light that each of us carries within each cell of our body and is released back into the universe when our physical body dies. And if we can light someone else's path along the way with love then it makes the world a less dark place and leads to an evolutionary change in the consciousness around us.

Printed in Great Britain
by Amazon